AFTER ATHEISM

SCIENCE, RELIGION AND THE MEANING OF LIFE

Mark Vernon

First published in hardback 2007

First published in paperback 2008 by
PALGRAVE MACMILLAN
Houndmills, Basingstoke, Hampshire RG21 6XS and
175 Fifth Avenue, New York, N. Y. 10010
Companies and representatives throughout the world

PALGRAVE MACMILLAN is the global academic imprint of the Palgrave
Macmillan division of St. Martin's Press, LLC and of Palgrave Macmillan Ltd.
Macmillan® is a registered trademark in the United States, United Kingdom
and other countries. Palgrave is a registered trademark in the European
Union and other countries.

ISBN-13: 978–0–230–01341–4 hardback
ISBN-10: 0–230–01341–4 hardback
ISBN-13: 978–0–230–01342–1 paperback
ISBN-10: 0–230–01342–2 paperback

This book is printed on paper suitable for recycling and made from fully
managed and sustained forest sources. Logging, pulping and manufacturing
processes are expected to conform to the environmental regulations of
the country of origin.

A catalogue record for this book is available from the British Library.

A catalog record for this book is available from the Library of Congress.

10 9 8 7 6 5 4 3 2 1
17 16 15 14 13 12 11 10 09 08

Printed and bound in Great Britain by
Antony Rowe Ltd, Chippenham and Eastbourne

For Nicholas George

CONTENTS

LIST OF ILLUSTRATIONS

The author and publishers have made every effort to contact copyright holders. If any have inadvertently been overlooked, the publishers will be pleased to make the necessary arrangements at the first opportunity.

ACKNOWLEDGEMENTS

A book like this is the product of many conversations and encounters, of many experiences and parts of life shared. Thank you and I look forward to more. In terms of producing the text, though, I want fulsomely to thank Jeremy Carrette, Paul Fletcher and Piers Benn who have read drafts and made suggestions. Needless to say, all faults remaining are mine. Great thanks are also due to Dan Bunyard at Palgrave as well as Lisa Dunn and my copy-editor, Peter Andrews.

Introduction

Our doubt is our passion.

Henry James

I USED TO BE A PRIEST. I trained for three years at an Anglican theological college. It was a dysfunctional institution that inspired and dismayed in turn. We excused it by saying that at least it was never luke-warm. Then, I worked as a clergyman in a high Church of England parish in the North East of England. It was a role with a clear sense of purpose being situated in a working-class community where, if much else had departed, the Church remained.

But mostly it was not a sense of social justice that made me don a dog-collar. Nor was I like those Christians who have a passion for conversion and a certainty that doctrine is as clear as the summer sky. I was ordained because I was gripped by what I can only call a religious imagination; the human spirit that cannot put meaning, beauty and transcendence - the very fact of existence - down. I loved the big questions. Friedrich Schleiermacher, the theologian, had stressed that religious feeling is pri-mary, dogmatics secondary: 'True religion is sense and taste for the Infinite,' he wrote. That made eminent sense to me. I felt drawn to another theologian, Paul Tillich, when he wrote that God was not a being, nor the monarch of monotheism, but was being-itself, the ground or power of being. The weightiness of such theology and the resonances of catholic liturgy mattered to me because I longed to connect with these mysteries. I took it that questing and doubts were more energising of an authentically religious outlook than any confessional formulations. And at the time of my ordination, buoyed up by the massive pillars and ancient sanctity of Durham cathedral, I found a certainty: God is love, love of life, and we in his Church are called to be lovers - I say that advisedly - too.

Illus. I.1:   Durham Cathedral has stood for over 900 years, 'half church of God, half castle 'gainst the Scot', as Sir Walter Scott put it.

This, I was to realise, is a sensibility that is profoundly felt but easily perturbed. The problem was that I could not say for certain how it all added up: how could it, when its object is God who is not an object or even ultimately a 'who'. So, in retrospect it is not surprising that disillusionment with God's earthly work set in too fast. The presenting symptoms for my crisis were loneliness in the job and frustration with the Church. Underneath that a number of neither coherent nor attractive objections raged. It depressed me that some clergy spent so much time policing their version of orthodoxy - monitoring who believed what about the Bible, the resurrection, homosexuality or women priests. It annoyed me that people wanted security from churchgoing more than challenge. The 'hatch, match and dispatch' routine that filled the week in between Sundays felt more like an industrial process than rites of passage. I was uncomfortable being an ambassador for a national organisation that seemed at least as hypocritical as it was helpful.

Against this background, the voices of theologians like Schleiermacher and Tillich came to seem irrelevant. They said that dogmatics should be derivative of the religious spirit, whereas the Church, in practice, seemed to do the reverse. So, I turned increasingly to humanist philosophers. 'Ah!', I began to think. Here is an account of things on the ground that is better than the double-talk of theology. Here is a discourse with edge. The threads of my faith thinned. And then snapped. Seeking succumbed to certainty. Doubts became a refusal of God. And now how I suspected that love-talk! It seemed like an excuse, like an opiate to cover epistemological realities. After a little less than three years in the Church, I quit. I had become a conviction atheist, a lover of the freedom and reason of the deicidal age.

It felt like growing up, like the history of humanity's conception of divinity played out in my own life. For centuries, people believed in many gods. Then, in a gradual process that began before Christ, tribal cultures mingled with each other and realised that their gods were like other gods: polytheism gave way to monotheism. And after that - and this, I now reckoned, was the genius of Christianity - God became man, which also meant that man had become God. Paradoxical though it may seem, with the birth of Christ, the death of God was only a matter of time. How lucky we are that this has been made manifest in our own age!

CULTURES OF CERTAINTY

Now, when Nietzsche announced the death of God, he told a story. A madman entered a marketplace where atheists were about their secular business. 'I seek God! I seek God!', he yelled - and they laughed. 'Is he hiding or on holiday?', they suggested in contempt.

For a while, after I left, I scoffed at believers too - until, that is, I noticed how Nietzsche continued. The crowd had the smirks wiped off their faces, for this madman was also a prophet. 'We are murderers,' he shouted, and proceeded to tell them what their killing had done. We think that we are now masters of the world, but we have actually unchained the sun, made our home cold, and strayed unawares into infinite space. 'Is not the greatness of this deed too great for us?', Nietzsche concluded. 'Must we ourselves not become gods simply to appear worthy of it?' Man as God: how impossible and laughable is that!

His point is that the death of God is not a triumph, it is a tragedy. And a while after my atheistic turn, I began to sense it. My newfound certainty crumbled because atheism, as much as religious conservatism, seemed to entail a poverty of spirit. Militant non-believers began to look as unappealing as the fundamentalists who do not do doubt.

Nietzsche foresaw this outcome too. If all can be explained by science, as is this Man-made-god's belief and hope, why have morality, values or spirit at all, he asked? If nature and history can be understood by mechanisms, rules and laws, then is not purpose, imagination and life inevitably sidelined and then squeezed out? Of course, in practice, even the fiercest atheist adopts some set of values that they superimpose on the world. It is impossible to live otherwise. They might even say that inventing, not inheriting, morality is part of the liberation, and ask if this is not what it means for humanity to know of God?

The trouble is that we are not divine. So this humanism can easily be made to look flimsy and challenged. It is why, I suspect, contemporary ethical discourse so often sounds like a repeat record. 'Freedom of speech, human rights, equality for all!' 'Freedom of speech, human rights, equality for all!' 'Freedom of speech, human rights, equality for all!' Yes, yes and yes! But to what end? On what basis? And why? The same thought exposes the emptiness of what often seems like modern life's sole goal, namely, the pursuit of technological progress. Many goods have arisen from the appliance of science. The trouble is that technology only nourishes us in certain ways. It can entertain us, but not make us happy. It can heal us, but not make us whole. It can feed us, but only in body. It offers defences, but does not make us feel secure. The double trouble is that technology is *so* good at this entertaining, healing, feeding and defending that it is easy to believe, or hope, that it can, or one day will, solve all other human ills too. Some say it might even makes us immortal - an apparent deification of humanity.

What is missing is meaning. Modern humanism finds it hard to address the questions of morality, values and spirit. Following the scientific rationalism it holds in high regard, it tends to boil it all down to a discussion of mechanisms, rules and laws. This may create an illusion of meaning and a sense of purpose. But meaninglessness keeps rearing its head because, well, mechanisms, rules and laws are actually not very meaningful. This is why atheism feels like a poverty of spirit. This is why 'Why?' is the cry of our age and we are no longer quite sure who we are. We are like Sisyphus: forcing the boulder of our values to the top of a mountain, hoping to lend them the authority of a high place, only to see them roll down again. In truth, this is absurd, as Camus realised - though only a few can stomach that thought. 'Thus wisdom wishes to appear most bright when it doth tax itself,' says Angelo in Shakespeare's *Measure for Measure*.

What is doubly distressing is that contemporary Christian discourse often sounds the same way too. It readily slips into being a process of mechanisms (being saved), rules (being good) and laws (being right). It was with the Copernican revolution that things began to change. The new science seemed to render many Christian conceptions of the universe unlikely or invalid. The Victorian age that followed was one in which belief struggled with disbelief and science seemed to be winning out. Hence, Nietzsche's announcement. What is overlooked, as I did at first, is that he also exposed science as bad religion - because it unchains the sun and floats unguided amongst the stars. So, science did not win conclusively. But it has been successful to the extent that it has altered the terms of debate. And having been thus challenged to prove itself, Christian orthodoxy tries to make itself look like a 'transcendental

science'. It used to be faith seeking understanding, now it is surety seeking expression; it was a search, it is now a statement. As one of the
founders of American fundamentalism, A. C. Dixon, declared: 'I am a
Christian because I am a Thinker, a Rationalist, a Scientist.' Thus, the
most successful examples of contemporary churchgoing are conservative
and evangelical. Even liberal churches have not escaped unscathed. They
are increasingly defined by what they are not against - be that being not
against homosexuality, women priests, contraception or divorce. What
they struggle to do is to articulate a sense of self on their own account.

Having lost faith with atheism, I could not simply go back to
Christianity. My scoffing at belief stopped but so had the appeal of belonging to a church. This was partly a matter of being sensible. A life lived
against the rising tide of conservatism, for the sake of an institution that I
could not help but regard as flawed, would not be healthy. It was also a
matter of being honest. The modern Church requires you to adhere to a
creed that is more substantial than God is love: one should really be able to
make a good stab at believing that God is Father, God is incarnate in
Christ, God is in his Church and God is revealed in the Bible. Hand on
heart, straight forwardly, I could not and can not. I once had a conversation,
walking down Oxford High Street, about whether the churches would ever
drop the recitation of their historic creeds. In that rarified atmosphere I
thought that this might be to advance the quest for God. Foolishly, it did
not occur to me that they are not called formularies for nothing.

Wittgenstein famously wrote, 'What we cannot speak about we must
pass over in silence.' For a while, after atheism, I thought I should be
silent too. If my journey had taught me anything, I reasoned, it was that
some things just cannot be said. But that did not last for long. It has also
been said that some people are not musical when it comes to religion.
Well it became apparent to me that I was. My religious imagination was
rekindled and I began to enjoy the big questions again. Like the operas
of Wagner, that I know one day I shall have to sit down and listen to, I
could not pretend that centuries of spirituality could be simply
discounted, as the flotsam and jetsam of more primitive times. The big
questions flourished for me once more.

But neither believer nor non-believer - a doubting Thomas, doubting
Richard Dawkins combi - where and how? My suspicion is that this

predicament, at least in outline, is a common one. Not only does it partially mirror the history of Western ideas over the last few hundred years, but I feel it must resonate with the many who are as dissatisfied with conservative belief as they are with militant disbelief. Around 40 per cent of Americans are not members of a church though say they do *not* simply not believe in God. And nearly a quarter of Britons frankly admit they are open and undecided.

ON BEING AGNOSTIC

We are what is called agnostics. Or to be more precise Christian agnostics. I think it is important to emphasise the 'Christian' for two reasons. First, it is in a Christian context that agnosticism as a question of rational assent typically comes about - not least because of the modern history of Christianity and science. In Eastern religions, being agnostic makes little sense since the form of these religions is so different. And in Judaism and Islam, religious systems that are in some ways close to Christianity, it seems more natural to talk of degrees of practice than belief. Second, it is better to talk of Christian agnosticism because the idea of God with which agnostics struggle (and which atheists deny) is Christian. It is monotheistic and shaped by the Christian tradition.

Agnostic - meaning 'not known' - was a word first coined by T. H. Huxley in 1869. A Victorian populariser of science, he found himself at the centre of the religious crisis sparked by the rise of science. The agnostic, Huxley said, is not an atheist but is someone who tries everything, and holds only to 'that which is good'. In an essay, entitled *Agnosticism*, he wrote:

> Positively the principle may be expressed: In matters of the intellect, follow your reason as far as it will take you, without regard to any other consideration. And negatively: In matters of the intellect do not pretend that conclusions are certain which are not demonstrated or demonstrable.

Huxley and others like him were passionate men, embroiled in debates with dogmatists of science and religion alike. Today, though, the word

8

Illus. I.2:   T. H. Huxley coined the word agnosticism saying that he was against 'gnosis' - doctrinaire knowing.

agnostic has come to mean something both less rational and more passive. Its strong sense - the considered conviction that nothing of ultimate things can be known with certainty - has been subsumed in the weak sense of someone who is simply non-committal or indifferent. This has happened because times have changed. In Huxley's day science had the upper hand, and Christianity was in retreat. Victorians had to struggle with what they might believe and what they should doubt, and with that struggle came their convictions - for or against or deliberately unsure. Today, though, someone can be agnostic with little more than a shrug of the shoulders. Like flat-pack goods, agnosticism can just click into place, part of the drab mental furniture of the theologically uninspired. I remember a flyer we were given at the start of the Oxford lecture course on the historical Jesus. It contained a list of what he can be known to have said for sure. It was not long. However, the real sadness was not that so little is known about Jesus, but that it takes so little effort to arrive at that conclusion today. This is inevitable, given the settled results of biblical criticism. But before it had established these results, there was something to be fought over, something to be passionate about. Similarly, the introduction to analytical philosophy course I attended had me doubting I was sitting on a chair in less than five minutes. It was an uncertainty that was so easy, it was boring.

WISDOM'S LOVERS

To put it another way, Victorian agnosticism was a way of seeing the world and a framework from which to approach life. The weak form of agnosticism that is at least its partial legacy today is no such practice, or barely a principle, but merely a tacit non-belief. This presents two challenges to someone who senses that agnosticism has more to offer than that. First, it is necessary to show that agnosticism still matters at an intellectual level. If it had work to do, so to speak, in the Victorian period - to challenge the excesses of religion and science - then we must identify what work it has to do today, and why that matters. Second, if agnosticism is to be an alternative to dogmatic scientific and religious worldviews, and not just a critique of them, it needs to move beyond being an intellectual exercise to become an ethos. A life lived according to the tenets of scientific empiricism or religious faith is a way of life based upon those beliefs, and not just an abstract creed. Similarly, agnosticism must prove itself to be more than a set of dry questions and expansive enough to become a positive commitment.

Questions then. Does agnosticism matter today, in the sense of being of consequence and carrying weight? Can it be a conviction and not just a shrug of the shoulders? Why should it be a stance that makes the dogmatists of faith and science sit up and take notice? And can it carry weight again for the contemporary passionate doubter?

The writings of the philosopher Kierkegaard suggest why it should matter to the unquestioning believer. For him, faith was a problem not because it was disproved but because it seemed so impossible. He develops this in his book *Fear and Trembling* around the quintessential figure of faith, Abraham. Why Abraham? Because when God asked him to sacrifice his son Isaac, as a test of faith, Abraham said yes. On every conceivable level, this 'yes' of faith was impossible for Kierkegaard.

> [W]hen I have to think about Abraham I am virtually annihilated. I am all the time aware of that monstrous paradox that is the constant of Abraham's life. I am constantly repulsed, and my thought, for all its passion, is unable to enter into it, cannot come one hairbreadth further. I strain every muscle to catch sight of it, but the same instant I become paralysed.

Agnosticism is the position from which Kierkegaard struggles with faith. The paradox is that it is his agnosticism that gives faith its meaning: he argued that doubt underpins faith, since it ensures that the believer really has faith and faith alone. He calls this the leap of faith. He knows that it would be the most remarkable, refined and extraordinary thing. That is why it is agonisingly out of reach. He therefore despises those who say they have it or, for that matter, simply dismiss it: if faith can turn water into wine, he quips, they would turn wine into water; they make a 'clearance sale' out of true religious convictions.

Kierkegaard is a prophet who challenges Christianity today as much as he did in his time. If modern belief judges itself according to the standards set by a fact-testing, relevancy-seeking scientific humanism, the challenge is to recover the agnosticism of the religious imagination - the exploration found in chapters 4 and 5 here. There is a negative and positive aspect to this. Negatively, I want to argue that being beholden to the scientific worldview distorts Christianity, and arguably other religions too. Positively, by exploring the apophatic tradition, as well as revisiting the so-called proofs of God along with issues like the problem of evil, I want to make the case that not knowing who God is - being radically agnostic - is essential to theology. It is more fundamental than anything positive that can be said about God. The general point is that the agnostic spirit and a religious way of life are one and the same thing. To lose the former is to lose the latter.

When it comes to science, I believe agnosticism is crucial - the argument of chapters 2 and 3. It is for those who are neither utopian about a technological future, nor Luddite about the achievements of the present. Negatively, the technological age needs a constant grasp of the limits of science, so that it does not put too much faith in it, and an agnostic attitude can provide that. Positively, agnosticism takes these limits as pointing beyond what science can comprehend to the persistent mysteries of life - aspects of existence that carry value and meaning, and are best captured and expressed in non-scientific ways. The hope is that these ways of talking can regain some of the authority that the scientific worldview tends to seek to monopolise. Moreover it seems to me that the reinvigoration of these other visions of reality is an increasing pressing need. In a society that faces what has been called an epidemic of ennui, and is on the verge of environmental crisis, it is not just more technology we need but *more than* technology.

It is said that a little learning is a dangerous thing, because the learned forget that their learning is little. A humanism of humility, not hubris, is what agnosticism struggles to put centre stage, in the belief that it nurtures right thinking. But what about the person commonly called agnostic - the individual without faith though not without a sense of the religious? How can agnosticism be made to be worth its salt, for, following Huxley and Kierkegaard, it must inspire passion and be a quest that can make for a life too?

Passion, quest and life. In Plato's dialogue the *Phaedrus*, the eponymous friend of Socrates asks the founder of Western philosophy a question. Where and how can he find truth? Phaedrus has an admiration for the orator Lysias, thinking him a great speech-maker and writer. He presumes that he is also, therefore, wise. Socrates replies that this is not right: 'To call him wise, Phaedrus, seems to me too much, and proper only for a god. To call him wisdom's lover - a philosopher - or something similar would fit him better.' This is someone who does not possess but lacks the wisdom they desire.

Socrates is talking about himself. He is a lover of limits, of being thrown onto the unknown. He is also someone who turned to philosophy having become disillusioned with the overreaching science of his times. And he is a man with a religious imagination. He is fascinated by the big questions of life. He understands the limits of being human, of standing in between the ignorant animals and the wise gods. The seminal moment in his career came with a message from an oracle. It told him that uncertainty is characteristic of the human condition, but that human beings need not be pig ignorant. They can understand their predicament by becoming conscious of what they do and don't know - by being wise agnostics. This is why Socrates calls himself a lover of wisdom, a philosopher. Moreover, being a philosopher added up not just to a legacy of thought but to a life that informed a civilisation. It mattered. So, might it be that by reflecting on the figure of Socrates, agnosticism can rediscover its passion and *raison d'être* today? Could his passionate doubt suggest a contemporary agnostic way of life? This is the matter that I pursue in the first chapter and return to again in chapters 6 and 7.

Throughout I reflect on my own experience too, partly in the hope that it illuminates what a committed agnosticism might be, partly because what I hope to convey is, again, not merely rational argument but the sense of something lived. In that spirit, we start with a life - the life of Socrates.

SOCRATES' QUEST:
THE BEGINNING OF WISDOM

I am very conscious that I am not wise at all.

Socrates

IF YOU HAD TO CHOOSE A SITE for the greatest oracle in the ancient world you would be hard pushed to beat Delphi. Sitting both confidently and precipitously on a ledge below the Phaedraides - the 'Shining Cliffs' - in central Greece, it looks like the vertiginous certainties must have felt to the people who sought Apollo's word there for over 1000 years. Today, a wide road, built for coaches, brings visitors up from the plain of Thebes. Its sleepy meander seems oblivious to the calamitous events that took place beneath the tarmac: 'there is no road away from Delphi', said Seneca, reflecting on Oedipus' attempt to flee the oracle's curse by the same route, only to kill his father on the way. But after an hour or so, you turn one final bend, and suddenly the telltale signs of broken pillars and a ticket office emerge from the cyprus trees.

All that remains of the Temple of Apollo itself are the foundations and a handful of resurrected columns that tantalisingly indicate where the portico and its famous inscriptions - 'Know Thyself' and 'Nothing in Excess' - once stood. The most recurrent feature on the site is that of the treasury building, mini-strongholds built by Greece's competing city-states to show off their wealth and strength. However, far from being an unromantic reminder that religion and politics merged with one another for the ancients, or that most of what so moved them has been lost, a visit does not disappoint.

14

Illus. 1.1: The ruins of Delphi, high on the slopes of the 'Shining Cliffs'.

Go at the end of the day, as the sun sets behind Mount Parnassos and throws yellow light onto the stones. Below is a valley flooded with olive trees that appear to flow westward onto the lowlands and, in the distance, the sparkling Gulf of Corinth. The hubbub of modern tourism lessens and the hubbub of past pilgrims re-emerges: it is easy to imagine everything from tawdry trinkets being bought in the stoa as personal mementos of a blessing to the machinations of the Hellenic heavyweights who came to what was a veritable United Nations in order to curry favour and win control.

It was to this place that Socrates' childhood friend, Chaerephon, came in the 430s BCE. First, he purified himself in the Castalian spring and paid a fee. Then, he bought a goat for sacrifice, over which was thrown a jug of cold water. The goat shuddered, for this was the sign that the oracle would respond to a question. Next, he had to wait for his lot to be drawn. And finally he was ushered into the holy chamber to speak with the Pythia. Sitting on a tripod, wearing a bay leaf crown, and, some say, sniffing the hallucinogenic vapours that drifted up from a cleft in the rock, she uttered the words that launched a quest that would shape a civilisation. 'Is anyone wiser than Socrates?' Chaerephon asked impulsively. 'No one is wiser,' she said.

SOLVING THE RIDDLE

Chaerephon returned to Athens, told his friend what the oracle had said, and awaited his response. Socrates was only in his mid-30s and yet he already had a considerable reputation in philosophy. Chaerephon must have thought that the endorsement of the oracle would not only be a huge confidence boost but, as the word got around, would propel him to his rightful place amongst the greats.

He could not have been more wrong. Socrates was profoundly disturbed. He could not accept what Chaerephon reported. The reason was that although his career had taken off, he already knew that human philosophy was strictly earthbound. His wisdom, such as it was, consisted in a growing sense that he was not wise. Like an observer of the night sky humbled by the immensity of the universe, his idea of philosophy was not of inevitable progress towards the bright stars of certainty and knowledge, but was a dawning awareness that the forces which shape the world stem from dark masses and unknown energies. He resisted the accolade because it smacked of hubris, the very thing that he suspected was going wrong with the philosophy and politics of the still newly democratic Athens.

But what then should he make of the oracle? The Pythia could be lying. Philosophy in Athens was a competitive business, with fortunes made or lost as reputations waxed and waned. It was not beyond the bounds of possibility that a rival Sophist had taken the opportunity to speak with an attendant priest. A suitably compliant chap might have 'interpreted' the oracle for Chaerephon. The rival's hope might have been that a divine declaration of Socrates' supremacy would make the young upstart look ridiculous.

More likely though the oracle was a puzzle. It must be put to the test. So Socrates decided he would search Athens to see if he could find someone who was wiser than he.

He went first to speak to Anytus, a well-known Athenian and rising political star. He was thought to be talented, and indeed thought himself very able. If Anytus proved wiser than Socrates, then the oracle would be refuted. He asked the politician questions about what was just and pious, and beautiful and good - standard fare for someone whose business was inspiring the masses in this most high-minded of cities. But Socrates discovered that Anytus' wisdom was flaky. Worse, he believed the myth of his own brilliance.

However, if the first test had failed, it did give Socrates a clue as to the meaning of the riddle. Anytus knew nothing worthwhile but thought he did. This differed from Socrates who knew he knew nothing. 'So I am likely to be wiser than he is to this small extent, that I do not think I know what I do not know.'

One fool does not condemn the whole political class, so Socrates went to speak with another politician, and another, systematically working his way through the leaders of the Assembly. No-one passed the test: 'I found that those who had the highest reputation were nearly the most deficient.' Moreover, mixed in with a growing distaste for the self-righteousness of politicians and mounting alarm at what it meant for the city, he noticed that he was becoming unpopular. The gadfly was emerging from his chrysalis and another dimension to the oracle's words was becoming clear. His search was starting to feel like a mission, to bring down the mighty from their Assembly seats.

Ancient Greek religion was unlike our own in many respects. In particular, it had no canonical texts, like the Bible, nor magisterium of priests to enforce doctrine. But one group of thinkers were particularly important in defining the limits of pious behaviour and what counted as orthodoxy, namely, the poets. The works of Homer and Hesiod were especially venerated. Their stories of courage and sayings on the virtues provided the canon-like texts of the day. Phrases like, 'Of all things, change is sweet', or, 'Friends have everything in common', littered debate as proof texts and reference points, much like public figures today cite truisms such as, 'People love freedom', or, 'Love thy neighbour'.

The poets were, in other words, another group of people one or more of whom might be wiser than Socrates. He certainly had some great poetic, comic and tragic contemporaries including Sophocles, Euripides and Aristophanes. So, having found politicians lacking, Socrates took to questioning these individuals. Again, he wanted to 'catch himself more ignorant'. He identified what he thought were the most meaningful and considered examples of their work and asked them about it. But he was disappointed. And further, he noticed that bystanders who happened to overhear them as they talked often offered better interpretations of the poems than the poets themselves. This led Socrates to think that their poetry was not bad *per se*; he was not a Philistine. Rather they confused their ability to use words with wisdom. 'I soon realised that the poets do not compose their poems with real knowledge, but by some inborn talent and inspiration, like seers and prophets who also say many fine things without any understanding of what they say.'

With the wisdom of politicians and poets proved wanting, Socrates next wondered whether the oracle was referring to a different kind of knowledge, that of artisans and professionals. After all, he reasoned, they know how to make things like shoes and how to do things like heal someone, matters about which he knew nothing. Surely, they would be wiser than he. He spoke to them too.

It turned out that Athenian craftsman were certainly good at their craft. But like the London taxi driver who has the Knowledge *and* an opinion on everything else, they made the mistake of thinking that an ability in one area meant they were knowledgeable about everything else too. A third group of people had been questioned and shown up for their ignorance.

But at last Socrates was getting it. 'Would I prefer to be as I am with neither their wisdom nor their ignorance, or to have both?' he asked himself. He would prefer to be as he was, not wise, but not ignorant of his lack of wisdom either. And with this realisation the riddle from the oracle was solved. He understood what it meant. 'This man among you, mortals, is wisest who, like Socrates, understands that his wisdom is worthless.'

PHILOSOPHICAL CREED

Today it is easy to think of Socrates as a champion of rationalism - a critical mind who was not truly appreciated for centuries, when the clouds of theism cleared, as someone recently put it. However, what can be gleaned of the historical Socrates, through Plato's appropriation of him, suggests that he was no such atheistic figure at all. Rather, he was a conviction agnostic.

Agnosticism about gods, that sometimes became or was interpreted as atheism, was one of the features of developments in fifth-century BCE Greece of which Socrates was part. Protagoras' book *On Gods* captured the mood. Its first sentence reads:

> About the gods I cannot say either that they are or that they are not, nor how they are constituted in shape; for there is much which prevents knowledge, the unclarity of the subject and the shortness of human life.

Protagoras veiled the gods with uncertainty. He also raised the prospect that human knowledge is relative: 'The measure of all things is man, for things that are that they are, for things that are not that they are not.'

Plato himself seems to have taken a more conservative view of religion. In the *Laws*, he writes:

> Nowadays some people don't believe in gods at all, while others believe they are not concerned about mankind; and there are

others - the worst and most numerous category - who hold that in return for a miserable sacrifice here and a little flattery there, the gods will help them to steal enormous sums of money and rescue them from all sorts of heavy penalties.

Plato objects to the wilful derision and self-centred trivialisation of religion because of the arrogance associated with both. He struggles at many points in his dialogues with what a proper conception of the gods might be. 'It is difficult to find out the father and creator of the universe, and to explain him once found to the multitude is an impossibility,' one of his interlocutors remarks. But he basically thought that respect for religion was good. At worst it was an attitude that resonated with human uncertainty.

Socrates too is presented as being in between the extremes of committed atheism and superstitious belief, though in a different way to Protagoras again. It seems he thought that a regard for religious practice was a good thing for human beings because of the way it focused on his central interest: how we might understand the nature of human ignorance - our status in between animals and gods. So this agnosticism left open questions about the nature and existence of divinities, because nothing much can be said about them. (Xenophon puts an argument about the existence of gods into Socrates' mouth in his *Memoirs of Socrates* but its purpose - in Xenophon's slightly clumsy way - is negative, to distance Socrates from the accusation of atheism. It clearly does not work as a proof.) Instead, Socrates' theology - his god-talk - seems to have been almost wholly conducted at the human level, around human limits. The value of the divine was to remind us of what lies entirely beyond us. As we shall see, this stance on religion coincided with his understanding of himself as a philosopher.

BEAUTIFUL PEOPLE

The story of Socrates questioning the people of Athens is the story of his emergence onto the public stage. It is told in the *Apology*, probably Plato's earliest dialogue and the one that is closest to the historical Socrates. The dialogue is a reconstruction of the speech Socrates made to defend himself at his trial. In it he also rehearses what was, in effect, his philosophical creed:

1. The human condition is one of uncertainty.
2. Reason coupled to an agnostic attitude are needed to understand that condition.
3. Human wisdom, such as it is, is a deep appreciation of the limits of understanding.
4. Self-knowledge is best gained with others and seeking it is to care for the soul.
5. The 'ignorant wise', who lack self-knowledge, shall be unsettled.

The creed caused him great difficulties for he was very good at undermining the security and wounding the vanity of his fellow citizens. We read that people thought talking to Socrates was like being stung by a ray. Others rapidly made themselves scarce when they saw him approach. If it was hard to tolerate for them it was hard for Socrates too. His new philosophical vocation rapidly became a source of danger to his person. The men he tended to upset the most were also the most powerful, and therefore the most violent and ambitious. They slandered him in ways that were hard for him to refute. At his trial, Socrates complains that they accused him of things that he himself despised. For example, they said that in debate he made 'the worse argument the stronger'. This was something the Sophists did, those professional know-it-alls who could be bought and who turned philosophy into a cockfight. To accuse Socrates of doing the same thing was to misunderstand him completely: he plumbed ignorance. They also said he sought meaning in the clouds (one of the surviving plays of Aristophanes is *The Clouds*, a harsh satire of what the comic took to be Socrates' nebulous philosophising). This was dangerous because it carried the implication of atheism, a position that whilst not unknown or overly shocking could become politically charged should someone choose to use it against you. After all Protagoras had only just escaped being executed when his agnosticism was misinterpreted in this way.

However, there was a silver lining to these dark clouds of unpopularity. Young men, especially rich, well-turned-out young men, with time on their hands, started to follow Socrates around Athens. For them, it was like knowing Mark Twain or Oscar Wilde: they hoped he would bump into someone of significance and make a mockery of them. And they loved him for it. At his trial he was also accused of corrupting youth, meaning turning them against their elders and betters.

Better yet, these youths began to realise that Socrates was serious. They soon sought him out not just for entertainment but because they thought they might learn something. Examples of this are found in the so-called Socratic dialogues of Plato, ones that Plato wrote early in his career so probably reflecting what he had learnt from his teacher and not yet wholly shaped as his own. With them we can drill down a little more into what this philosophy of ignorance meant in practice.

Take the *Lysis*. It begins with Socrates out and about in Athens. He is walking between the Academy and the Lyceum, and, at the invitation of two young men, Hippothales and Ctesippus, he stops just outside the city walls - perhaps near the present-day excavations of Kerameikos. They want him to join them in their discussions by a newly built gymnasium. Gymnasia were a favourite haunt of Athenian youths. In this one the statuesque Lysis was exercising, someone on whom Hippothales had a massive crush. In the dialogue, Socrates spots it immediately, albeit no great feat since Hippothales blushed at the merest thought of his beloved. What is interesting for us, though, is that Socrates tells Hippothales that he has a remarkable ability to spot when someone is in love, and the person with whom he is smitten.

What did Socrates mean by this? It is, in fact, directly related to what he discovered about himself after grappling with the words of the oracle. He is a lover (*philia*) of wisdom (*sophia*), like Hippothales is a lover of Lysis; both lack what they desire. So his comment, which is repeated in other dialogues too, provides an insight into how Socrates must have felt, not just thought, about his calling as a philosopher. At times it ached. Hence the reason Socrates can spot lovers: he has an immediate sympathy with them (this seems likely to have been another reason why he got on so well with young men). It also shows that although Socrates was convinced the human lot was riven through and through with uncertainty, it did not mean he lacked passion. He was not like the agnostic who shrugs their shoulders with indifference. Rather, the lack of wisdom made his heart grow all the fonder of it. Like Romeo who gasps, 'Did my heart love 'till now?', at the merest thought of Juliet, Socrates longed for what he lacked. His ignorance, and knowledge of his ignorance, powered a relentless desire for the truth about himself, his fellows, and the verisimilitudes of the world around him.

There is a second dimension to this philosophical love that comes out in the encounter too. Socrates is drawn to others, not only because of his sympathy but also because it is with others that he gains the best understanding of himself, and they of themselves. This is again implicit in his reaction to the oracle. He did not test himself on his own, as a modern recipient of such words might do, perhaps by trying to write a book. Rather he went out onto the streets. As Plutarch later put it:

> Socrates did not set up grandstands for his audience and did not sit upon a professorial chair; he had no fixed timetable for talking or walking with his friends. Rather he did philosophy sometimes by joking with them, or by drinking or by going to war or to the market with them ...

This meant that Socrates got to know people, and the better he got to know them, and they he, the better the philosophy. So philosophy for Socrates was not just about exploring ideas but was about understanding how people are the way they are. He believed the key to wisdom was self-understanding as well as defining abstractions. He had to get to know others to see if they were wiser than he was, a test that puts character as well as cleverness under the spotlight. In addition, it is an approach that recognises that intuition is on a continuum with reason. How we implicitly react to things should count alongside how we explicitly rationalise them. As Wordsworth realised, thoughts are 'representatives of our past feelings'.

When it really worked, this was a process of befriending: 'I think that someone who is to test adequately the soul which lives aright and the soul which does not, needs to have three qualities: knowledge, goodwill and willingness to speak freely,' Socrates once said to one of his interlocutors. Alternatively, in the *Lysis*, he later confesses that he would rather have a friend than anything else in the world, even more than all the gold of the Great King. Why? Because with such a friend he would understand himself: they would be perfect mirrors to each other and, in that mutual trust, would know each other as well as they knew themselves.

LIVING UNCERTAINTY

This picture of Socrates' philosophy can be developed some more by considering further his engagement with the Delphic oracle. Ancient oracles are much misunderstood today. It is easy to think of them as a kind of cryptic fortuneteller or sophisticated roller of dice. But they are more fascinating than that. Whilst no doubt they could be corrupted and ridiculed, at heart they were a system for decision making in a world very conscious that nothing could be predicted, much was up to luck, and everything was uncertain. Consulting the oracle, and receiving equivocal replies, did three things. It dramatised the experience of not knowing. It impelled the work of interpretation. It called all possibilities into question.

Consider two of the most famous consultations at Delphi. A first was when Croesus, the king of Lydia, sought the oracle's blessing on his proposed war against Persia. The Pythia uttered the words: 'A great empire will be destroyed.' In his hubris, Croesus took the empire to be that of his enemy. It was, in fact, that of his own. Now, the cynic would respond to this by saying that the oracle always has the last laugh: it speaks in ways that can be re-interpreted after the event. But that, I think, would be a misunderstanding. Ancient people too knew that oracles must be doubted. Croesus himself had previously tested all the major oracles of the ancient world by asking them what he would be doing at a certain time on a future day. Only Delphi got it right (cooking lamb and tortoise in a bronze pot, as it happens). It is as if the very triviality of that prediction emphasised the effort you should go to when considering what the oracle says on matters as serious as going to war. Had Croesus seen through his pride, and heard not endorsement but different possibilities implicit in the oracle's words, he would have stared the unpredictability of war in the face, and perhaps saved the lives of his people.

A similar lesson was missed by the Roman Appius. As civil war was looming, at what we now know to be the end of the Roman republic, he asked the oracle about his future. The Pythia said he will 'escape the awful threats of war' and 'stay at peace in Euboea'. Appius took this to be consoling; he would not die and so need not fear the horrors that internecine carnage brings. But, again, had he allowed the words to sink in properly, he would have detected an ambivalence. It might mean he avoided the war. But it might also mean that he would die before war broke out - which is exactly what happened. He thought he had cheated death, but it was death that brought him peace in Euboea.

Every part of the oracle experience, then, gave cause to pause and reconsider. It represented not the sleep of reason but the opposite, the call to wake reason up. It began with the effort of the journey to the shrine. Delphi was high in the hills. Siwa, the oracle Alexander the Great consulted about his parentage, was several days ride into the middle of the western Egyptian desert. Next there was the preparation and ritual, coupled to the risk that the oracle might not speak. Finally, if the oracle did oblige, what had been said had then to be resolved, for the proper way to hear it was to dwell on its ambiguity and generate its meaning. As was the case with Socrates, being ambivalent about an oracle was not to question its truth so much as to struggle with its significance. To borrow a phrase from Wittgenstein, the issue was how its language 'hooks onto the world'. The experience was like a therapy that could transform blind action - deluded or devoid of self-knowledge - into wise action.

In some ways it did not even matter what the oracle said. Oracles were not designed to issue laws or edicts. They gave signs, that the wise pondered greatly. Like paying an expert today, the real benefit might not be in the advice itself so much as in the commitment to the consultation process. The oracle/consultant says 'x' and 'not x', and thereby sets an agenda. The advice provides an authoritative, unsettling point of reference that can then be talked around.

Even to those who would say it is folly, the oracle might reply, 'well, yes'. It instantiates the folly of seeking certainty in life. Its 'unknown unknowns' put human credulity centre stage. Instead, it suggests a path in between a believer's certainty and an unbeliever's cynicism that simultaneously mirrors the 'in-between' reality of the human condition. Little wonder that Socrates should come to appreciate the fulness of his vocation through the voice of an oracle. In terms of the experience, an oracle is not unlike his philosophy.

KNOW THYSELF

The oracle can tell us more about Socrates still. Consider the two inscriptions on the temple at Delphi. They were said to encapsulate the wisdom of the Seven Wise Men, a traditional if variable list of the most outstanding intellects of ancient Greece, usually including Thales, the first philosopher. 'Nothing in excess' is generally taken as advocating moderation. 'Know thyself' meant 'know you are not a god before you enter this temple'. What Socrates does is internalise these commands and transform them from warnings into a quest. 'Nothing in excess' comes to commend a moderate regard for oneself. 'Know thyself' becomes the imperative to understand yourself. In these two maxims one finds another summary of his philosophy. They pose the question of how one can know oneself and highlight how hard it is to understand and accept the uncertainty of the human condition. For if the human condition is one of uncertainty, then the question, 'who am I?', is frightening. It is elusive and will never, finally, be settled. It is for this reason that the 'how' of knowing oneself often gives way to the 'how' of 'how should one live?' The letter's practicalities provide comfort in the face of daunting existential crisis.

The ancients, it seems, were fascinated by this second question. Evidence of popular tips, perhaps not entirely unlike those that can be found in glossy magazines, survive for us to inspect. One papyrus found in the ash-covered town of Herculaneum, neighbour to Pompeii, records a 'four-part cure' from anxiety: (1) Don't fear god; (2) Don't worry about death; (3) What is good is easy to get; (4) What is terrible is easy to endure. This is a summary of Epicureanism, one of the ancient philosophies to develop a genuinely popular following. But notice how the four-part cure begs a question: 'how should one live?' will never be fully answered unless the prior question of 'who am I?' is.

Socrates suspected that it was not only glossy magazines, as it were, that could fail to address the real question. He thought that any form of written philosophy risked doing so too. That is why he did not write anything in his own hand. Wisdom cannot be read off the page, or, as Plato put it, it is not like water that can be poured from one vessel into another. The point is that reading philosophy can be as much of a distraction as following four-part cures and the like: it can pose as philosophy without touching on the crucial matter of self-understanding.

> I have no time for such things; and the reason, my friend, is this. I am still unable, as the Delphic inscription orders, to know myself; and it really seems to me to be ridiculous to look into other things before I have understood that. This is why I do not concern myself with them. I accept what is generally believed, and, as I was just saying, I look not into them but into my own self.

Am I a beast, Socrates continues in this section of the *Phaedrus*, or do I have a divine nature? - again recalling the in-between status of what it is to be human. This, then, is how Socrates tries to ask the question. Knowing oneself becomes a matter of developing the right attitude to oneself and the world around one. This care for oneself too becomes part of his philosophy.

All in all, Socrates' agnostic enquiry became a committed way of life. What had started as a puzzle from the oracle was now a total philosophy. It was a quest that deployed reason as a tool, to test the limits of what people really knew: scholars today talk of Socrates' method, the so-called elenchus - meaning the drawing out of the consequences of a position or belief to see whether they are contradictory or inconsistent. But Socrates was also conscious that reason has limits. Like a pianist who quickly learns that technique is only the start of making music, Socrates learnt that reason is far from the whole of life. Reason does much of the ground work - notably alerting you to your ignorance. After that the development of matters as diverse as character and intuition, your circle of friends and the cultivation of what you love, and the challenge of the Delphic imperatives, must also play their part.

ARE GODS GOOD?

But even all these elements do not capture the whole of his philosophy. There is a religious dimension to incorporate too. His references to the gods were a pervasive and subtle part of his makeup, made all the difference to his philosophy, and are as important as the personal and political aspects of his life. If reason is the beginning of wisdom, it seems that he thought a religious sense is what draws it out.

Consider one of Socrates' most famous theological arguments, found in another dialogue, the *Euthyphro*. It tells the story of Socrates' conversation with a young man, after whom the dialogue is named, and takes place in front of the magistrates courts in the marketplace. Euthyphro had come there to prosecute a charge of murder, and no ordinary murder, but one allegedly committed by his father. What is even more startling about the case is that the person whom his father had supposedly killed was only a slave. What had happened was that this slave had himself killed another slave in a drunken rage. Euthyphro's father had bound the offender and dumped him in a ditch. However, he had then forgotten about him and, left there, the slave died of exposure. Euthyphro is a puritanical young man who feels his father must be brought to justice to cleanse what he considers to be a stain on his family. And this is what interests Socrates. Socrates thinks that for Euthyphro to pursue such a headline-grabbing case, he must be very sure that the moral benefit he would gain from the prosecution would not be outweighed by the offence of dishonouring his father. In short, Euthyphro is acting dogmatically - as if he has very certain knowledge of what it means to be pious.

Euthyphro argues that he is right to prosecute his father because he believes that the gods denounce murderous acts. This is what makes the crime so bad. Socrates is fascinated by this assumption. In it, he sees a more general thesis: what is good is what the gods love. And, conversely, what is wrong is what the gods hate. Moreover, thinks Socrates, this thesis raises a wider question still. Is what is good loved by the gods because it is good, or is it good because it is loved by the gods?

Euthyphro is slightly confused by this point. So Socrates helps him out. Consider, he says, whether saying something is good is like saying something is seen. Something that is seen depends on someone seeing it. So is something being good dependent upon someone, like a god, saying it is good? Euthyphro thinks this cannot be right, since the good is good because it is good, not because of any feelings someone, even a god, might have for it. Socrates tends to agree.

The reason this debate is remembered is that many modern philosophers have taken it as profoundly undermining of theistic belief. It suggests that what is good is prior to anything a deity may say about it, which not only implies that the deity is subject to something over which it has no options, but that morally speaking we do not need theism to tell us what is good. The standard, theistic reply to this conclusion is that God is goodness itself. The atheist's argument is flawed, theists say, because it suggests that there is some kind of separation between the virtue and the divinity which in the case of God there is not. But, replies the atheist, you cannot escape the fact that you say God is good because God has the properties of goodness. In which case, you should be able to list the properties of goodness without reference to God. And so the argument goes round and round.

What is interesting about the original account of it in the *Euthyphro* though is that Socrates does not pose any arguments like this at all. It apparently never occurs to him, or Euthyphro, that the dilemma is a challenge to the gods. This could be put down to a number of things. Perhaps the pressing matter in the dialogue is not whether the gods exist but whether Euthyphro should prosecute his father. Though the conversation broadens out in other ways, so why not in this direction? Alternatively, it might be thought that Socrates lived in a society in which the existence of the gods was basically beyond question; ancient Athenians did not experience the world as disenchanted as we, it is said, do today. But, as already described, agnostic and atheistic ideas did circulate in ancient Athens, so it is significant that Plato does not choose to make something of them here.

I think that Socrates does not see the dilemma as troubling vis-à-vis the gods because of his conviction about the uncertainty of the human condition. This implies, first, that he thinks that no-one, with any seriousness, can presume to know what may or may not cause a divinity a sleepless night. And, second, it implies that what is far more obvious to him is that the dilemma should be troubling to human beings. Whatever it may be to be a god, it is human beings who must grapple with what it means to be good, not them. (Socrates would be concerned about the assumption behind the modern atheist's reply that the properties of goodness can be listed. What are these properties of goodness, he would ask; tell me that and you are a wiser man than I.)

The dialogue ends inconclusively. Euthyphro is troubled by Socrates' line of thought, but rather than trying to come to terms with what it might mean for his dogmatism, he hurries off, stung. Whether he continued with the prosecution of his father we do not know. We can, though, ponder some more of what it suggests about Socrates' approach to theology and how that connects with his way of life.

First, it implies that Socrates was not very interested in debates about whether gods exist or not. Perhaps he suspected that when conducted as a knock-out between a theist and an atheist they go nowhere fast. Having said that, he was interested in theological debate: if god-talk can avoid getting hung up on 'proofs', then it can become a way of critiquing human knowledge. Examining what people take to be divine is valuable because it reminds them that they are made lower than gods and that aspirations to god-like knowledge will remain just that - aspirations. Then, if this can be stomached, the attitude it nurtures itself becomes a valuable source of insight, for religious humility is the product of embracing the human condition. With it, the vain attempt to 'overcome' is ditched, and the challenge to understand is taken on. And this, in turn, is what makes life worthwhile. It produces the best kind of human beings, people who are not merely ignorant, but recognise the ways in which they are. To this extent, they become wise and lovers of wisdom. To put it another way, the unexamined life is not worth living, negatively because it would be deluded, and positively because examining all those other things in life - character, intuition, friendships, loves and fundamentally 'who am I?' - gives life shape and meaning. (Conversely, Socrates quips, gods cannot be 'philo-sophers' for the very reason that they possess divine knowledge - taking a dig at the philosophers who would become gods.)

MARGINAL BELIEF

To the extent that he reframed theology as an anthropocentric activity Socrates was heterodox for his times. Consider the issue of the gods and goodness again. It was common to regard the gods as somewhat arbitrary when it came to the goodness of their deeds. When Zeus and his wife Hera argued on Mount Olympus, Zeus would do a monstrous thing one day and Hera some good, and then, after an argument the next day, Zeus would do the good thing and Hera some horror. Who could tell how it might turn out? Similarly, when a city-state sought the assistance of its divinities in times of war, the plea was not the modern-day sentiment 'our cause is right', with the implication that God must be on our side. Rather it was 'you owe it to us', because of all the sacrifices your citizens have performed for you.

Socrates rejects these ideas. Quite reasonably he thought that if we can see that the actions of Zeus and Hera are arbitrary and unjust then they as gods must be able to see that too. So they cannot be like that to start with. That they are popularly taken to be so smacks of human mistake. Similarly, on the matter of bargaining with the gods, Socrates thought that whatever the heavenly realm might be like it must be one of moral consistency and divine harmony. So, whatever it might be to communicate with the gods, it is ridiculous of people to think that they can be bargained with. This was actually a far more dangerous idea than straightforward atheism. It implied that one city-state, like Athens, might not have the gods on its side when pitted against an enemy, like Sparta, that did.

Having said that, Socrates is depicted in Plato's dialogues as being quite conventional in his religious practice. He makes sacrifices, attends feasts, pours libations, offers prayers and pursues oracles. Partly, he seems to have believed that religious practice should be respected since it opens the mind and cultivates the agnostic attitude; it is an exercise in intellectual humility. Partly, he is acknowledging that reason alone is limited and that for all someone might be influenced by rational argument, the care of soul - the holistic aim of his philosophy - clearly takes more than sound logic.

INNER DAEMONS

There is another aspect of Socrates' religious sensibility that we cannot pass over - simply because of the number of times that Plato and others refer to it. This is what Socrates calls his *daimonion* or daemon. 'It's a voice that, when it comes, always signals me to turn away from what I'm about to do, but never prescribes anything.' Although the voice is intimate and only ever heard by Socrates, he was well known for it: the charge of introducing new gods that he faced at his trial probably referred to this suspiciously private apparent access to the divine.

What the daemon tells Socrates not to do ranges from the trivial to the life-threatening. Most often, it tells him simply to sit down when he is about to stand up, usually so as not to miss an encounter with others who are about to pass by. Sometimes it offers similarly negative advice for others: it once told Socrates to tell Charmides, Plato's handsome but tyrannical uncle, not to train for a race at Nemea, an ancient Olympic contest that involved running 200 km in just over a day. Much more seriously, Socrates believed he was obeying his daemon when he stayed in Athens to drink the hemlock. He could have easily got away.

What are we to make of Socrates' daemon? It is actually probably wrong to think of it as a voice, as if it were a guardian angel or some kind of internal conversation with himself. The Greek *daimonion* expresses uncertainty - Socrates does not know whence it comes or whither it goes - and strangeness, as if it were a force or urge that, if familiar, he fails to understand.

In the *Symposium*, there are two incidents that enlarge on this. The first occurs when Socrates meets a priestess, called Diotima. They had a conversation in which Diotima explained who or what Eros (Love) is. Socrates had assumed up to that point that Eros was divine. But no, says Diotima. Eros is a daemon, an entity that exists in between the heavenly realms and human society. The gods 'mingle and converse' with humans by these daemons, she says, mostly when people sleep, or for some when they are awake - a process that Plato elsewhere alludes to as 'yearning after and perceiving something, it knows not what'.

Eros is a particularly interesting daemon because of his origins. When Aphrodite was born, the gods held a party. Poros (meaning 'way'), son of Metis (meaning 'cunning') was there, got drunk and fell asleep in the garden. Meanwhile, Penia (meaning 'poverty') passed by, and discerning a cunning way out of her poverty, slept with Poros and became pregnant. Eros was the result.

Diotima continues her story by describing Eros in more detail, and she does so in ways that exactly match Socrates. Both are poor, ugly and shoeless. Both long for something they lack, but are endlessly cunning in the pursuit of what they love - divine wisdom. Thus, concludes Diotima: 'He is in between wisdom and ignorance as well.' The message is clear.

Illus. 1.2:   Socrates' ugly appearance accentuated the inner beauty of his
unsettling wisdom.

Socrates' daemon is like eros: it is a go-between for an in-between, and is another manifestation of the way his philosophy drives him like love.

The second incident comes after Socrates and Diotima have finished speaking, when Socrates' sometime pupil Alcibiades, now an Athenian leading light, comes in. He proceeds to give a speech in praise of Socrates, though as it turns out it is as much a rant - not least when describing the disturbing, daemonic effect Socrates has on him:

> I swear to you the moment he starts to speak, I am beside myself: my heart starts leaping in my chest, the tears come streaming down my face, even the frenzied Corybantes seem sane compared to me - and I tell you, I am not alone. I have heard Pericles and many other great orators, and I have admired their speeches. But nothing like this ever happened to me: they never upset me so deeply that my very own soul started protesting that my life - my life! - was no better than the most miserable slave's. He always traps me, you see, and makes me admit that my political career is a waste of time, while all that matters is just what I most neglect: my personal shortcomings that cry out for my closest attention. So I refuse to listen to him; I stop my ears and tear myself away from him, for, like the Sirens, he could make me stay by his side till I die.

Notice how it is not just Socrates' rational challenges that causes Alcibiades to doubt everything. It is a psychological force that he wields and that causes so much distress. This force brings Alcibiades' political aspirations into question and his deepest, darkest motivations. What he describes is a complete collapse of self-confidence - 'my heart, or my soul, or whatever you want to call it, has been struck and bitten by philosophy', he continues. Again, a clear message about Socrates is being given. Socrates' daemon calls into question every part of life. In this, it is intimately connected to his philosophy.

SOCRATES IN CONVERSATION

Bertrand Russell called himself an agnostic, though one who was 'atheistically inclined'. This is different from the agnosticism of Socrates.

If Russell's agnosticism made him tend towards atheism, Socrates' agnosticism made him want to hold onto god-talk and religious practice. It richly reflected his conviction of the in-between status of human beings. In a magazine called *Look*, published in 1953, Russell clarified what agnosticism meant for him. He was asked a series of questions. There is, perhaps, some benefit in juxtaposing exerpts from some of the answers he gave with ones Socrates might have given. The conversation defines, as it were, two poles on the continuum of agnostic belief.

What is an agnostic?

Russell: An agnostic is a man who thinks that it is impossible to know the truth in the matters such as God and a future life with which the Christian religion and other religions are concerned. Or, if not for ever impossible, at any rate impossible at present.

Socrates: I too have never found anything but uncertainty in divine matters, but that is not a good reason for outright unbelief. For one thing, the same seems true in human matters. My agnostic is someone who is religiously minded but without the same commitment, or what you would now call faith, of the believer.

Are agnostics atheists?

Russell: No. An agnostic suspends judgement ... At the same time, an agnostic may hold that the existence of God, though not impossible, is very improbable; he may even hold it so improbable that it is not worth considering in practice.

Socrates: No - but not because it is not worth considering in practice. I do find many of the dogmatic convictions of believers unlikely, but I am very drawn to talk about theological things; it leads to a modest regard for oneself the value of which cannot be underestimated when it comes to what one does in practice.

Since you deny 'God's law', what authority do you accept as a guide to conduct?

Russell: An agnostic does not accept any 'authority' in the sense in which religious people do. He holds that a man should think out questions of conduct for himself.

Socrates: We should certainly try to think out questions of conduct for ourselves. But that does not exclude respecting any higher authority. Sometimes we must, for we cannot decide everything for ourselves.

Does an agnostic deny that man has a soul?

Russell: The question has no precise meaning unless we are given a definition of the word 'soul'. I suppose what is meant is, roughly, something non-material which persists throughout a person's life and even, for those who believe in immortality, throughout all future time. An agnostic is not likely to believe that a man has a soul.

Socrates: I do not understand this objection to the idea of a soul - though it is no doubt hard to pin down. Must we not take care of our souls, in our character and imagination, and nothing is more beautiful than a soul growing wings and flying high. It must be to do with knowing ourselves, our intuitions and character - what emerges when we talk seriously.

Are you ever afraid of God's judgement in denying him?

Russell: Most certainly not. I observe that a very large portion of the human race does not believe in God and suffers no visible punishment in consequence. And, if there was such a God, I think it very unlikely that he would have such an uneasy vanity as to be offended by those who doubt his existence.

Socrates: I understand Professor Russell's concern with divine vanity; Homer is full of it. But, then, that is our issue not the gods'. So, if pushed, I'd say that, although divine judgement is beyond our comprehension, it must be what we call justice. And, since this justice is so elusive, we can only gain from trying to align our souls to what we imagine a god's judgement must be. So, yes, I am afraid of divine judgement.

How do agnostics explain the beauty and harmony of nature?

Russell: I do not understand where this 'beauty' and 'harmony' is supposed to be found. Throughout the animal kingdom, animals

CARDIFF
CAERDYDD

ruthlessly prey upon each other ... I suppose the questioner is thinking of such things as the beauty of the starry heavens. But one should remember that stars every now and then explode ... Beauty, in any case, is subjective and exists only in the eye of the beholder.

Socrates: Beauty is certainly in the eye of the beholder. But, if I may say so, Professor, although I know nothing, there is one thing I am good at: spotting those who are in love. Your agnosticism seems to make you very wary about what you love. But love, even mad love, is what leads us to those things that are truly beautiful.

What is the meaning of life to the agnostic?

Russell: I feel inclined to answer by another question: what is the meaning of 'the meaning of life'? I suppose what is intended is some general purpose. I do not think that life in general has any purpose. It just happened. But individual human beings have purposes, and there is nothing in agnosticism to cause them to abandon these purposes.

Socrates: When death hangs over your head, the meaning of life is not academic, believe me! It is not found in the opinion of the many and what is important is not life but a good life. But even that takes us only so far. For myself, and though I do not always understand it, I have the blessing of what can only be called a keen religious sensibility that is founded upon the conviction that we must understand how we are ignorant. This leads me to pursue what is good and true and this is what life means to me.

Is faith in reason alone a dangerous creed?

Russell: No sensible man, however agnostic, has 'faith in reason alone'.

Socrates: We can agree on that!

Unlike the orthodox believer, Socrates' uncertain attitude undermines any certain beliefs. Unlike the committed atheist (or 'near' atheist), his questioning sensibility remains open to what god-talk might reveal about the in-between human condition. Socrates is religious because he is a committed passionate agnostic.

LAST WORDS

Socrates achieved something that only a handful of humans in history achieve; he changed the consciousness of a civilisation. 'We cannot fail to see in Socrates the one turning point and vortex of so-called world history,' said Nietzsche, who, as frequently, wished he *could* fail to see Socrates at the vortex of history. The purpose of putting the figure of Socrates at the beginning of this book is that the complex agnostic inspiration behind his philosophy is often forgotten today. The rich ambiguities that characterised his philosophical way of life are belittled by the hard-and-fast demands of the rationalist outlook. Its subtle grays are lost amidst the blacks and whites of thought abstracted from life.

In 399 BCE, Socrates was found guilty of not recognising the city gods, introducing new deities and corrupting the young. He was sentenced to death. Scholars have debated ever since whether Socrates was guilty of these things or whether an amalgam of unfortunate political association, presumed philosophical atheism, and stinging his enemies one too many times were the real causes. Probably it was a mixture of all three and Socrates' agnosticism was right there at the heart of it, disquieting his opponents.

A month of so later he drank the hemlock and died. His last words were: 'Crito, we owe a cock to Asclepius; pay it and don't forget' - not, at first glance, overly inspiring, though, as is the way with last words, they have been much reflected upon. Asclepius was one of the gods of healing; the sacrifice of a cock was a thanksgiving for overcoming illness. Socrates' last concern was, then, religious, and, once again, he turns conventional piety around: he was not going to live but was about to die. Was Plato's point merely rhetorical, saying he was pious to the last, for all that his accusers said otherwise? Nietzsche interpreted the last words as Socrates' giving thanks for the final escape from the sickness which is life itself, an idea he hated since it was the opposite of his 'will to power'. Alternatively, they might make sense if Socrates hoped he was

about to leave this in-between life and be cured of its ignorance. We cannot say for sure, not least because elsewhere Socrates says he is not sure
whether there is an afterlife, let alone whether he is sure what that afterlife might be like. So his agnosticism is echoed in his last words too -
giving thanks, as his humility would, though exactly to whom and for
what he knew not.

COSMOLOGISTS AND DARWINISTS:
THE LIMITS OF SCIENCE

One of the most painful circumstances of recent advances in science is that each one of them makes us know less than we thought we did.

Bertrand Russell

IF YOU THINK OF ISAAC NEWTON what image comes to mind? Is it an upright man with Restoration curls who, prism in hand, calmly explains the splitting of light to an attentive audience? Is it a dishevelled sage with tatty cuffs who, lost in thought under a tree, is hit by a falling apple and - eureka!? Is it a desiccated don who, prowling the cloisters like a wild beast, has reduced everything to an equation in his masterpiece, the *Principia*? Or is it a sulphur-soiled alchemist who, half mad with mercury poisoning, distills reason as a mere byproduct of the true search for the elixir of life?

The empiricist philosopher, David Hume, preferred something like the first: 'In Newton this island may boast of having produced the greatest and rarest genius that ever rose for the ornament and instruction of the species,' he wrote in his *History of England*. The romantic idea of genius is represented by the second image. It sees the apple as emblematic of the sudden moment of radical breakthrough: 'A ripe fruit fall from some immortal tree/ Of knowledge ... ', wrote the poet Alfred Noyes. The third, more ambivalent image is perhaps more like Keats who sighed, 'Do not all charms fly/ At the mere touch of cold philosophy?'.

And finally, there is Newton the alchemist, the man who worried more about crucibles and symbols than calculus and science. 'Newton was not the first of the age of reason. He was the last of the magicians, the last of the Babylonians and Sumerians, the last great mind which looked out on the visible and intellectual world with the same eyes as those who began to build our intellectual inheritance rather less than 10,000 years ago,' declared John Maynard Keynes, who saved many of Newton's alchemic manuscripts from destruction.

The evolution of the iconography of Newton, which Patricia Fara charts in her book *Newton: the Making of Genius*, is simultaneously a reflection of changing attitudes to science. That Newton's image varies so much, and on occasion is so fiercely contested, is indicative of the way the meaning of science has itself been contested in the 300 years since his death. Not unlike the figure of Socrates, there are, on the one hand, the rational materialists for whom any rehearsal of Newton's hermetic 'superstitions' is broadly irrelevant and vaguely offensive. Then, on the other hand, there are the romantic New Ageists in whose mouths the same rehearsal is meant as a condemnation of science as it has become.

But why, specifically, was Newton so interested in alchemy? What purpose did it serve in relation to his undoubted scientific achievements? Why did one of the greats of mathematics think of himself in 'the noble Companie of true Students in holy Alchimie'?

THE DARK GLASS

There are those who would say it was extraneous. Perhaps like Schopenhauer's long walks, Glenn Gould's tuneless humming, or Van Gogh's self-mutilation, alchemy was for Newton the excess of genius, a forgivable indulgence, a means of relaxation. There are others who say it was instrumental. For them, Newton's alchemy was in the service of his work at the Royal Mint. It was the way that research into metallurgy was done in those days; for 'alchemy' one should really read 'coin milling technology'.

However, the most recent scholarship demonstrates substantial links between Newton's alchemic experiments and theoretical achievements. A good example is provided by his fascination with comets. Today, this is usually remembered in relation to Newton's friend, Edmond Halley. He was the first to use the new laws of gravity to predict when the eponymous

Illus. 2.1:   Sir Isaac Newton - gentleman, sage, rationalist or alchemist?

comet, and 23 others, would return - which they did. However, for Newton, comets were fascinating not just because they appeared in the sky but because the intermittency of their appearing resonated with his view of God. His was a deity who intermittently intervened in the universe. So, he conjectured, might the impact of a comet on earth have been the cause of divine interventions like Noah's flood?

Another example of his interplay of religion and science is found in the way Newton thought about the mysterious action of gravity at a distance. He postulated that the universe was filled with a tenuous ether. This ether served two purposes. First, being made of tiny particles, it could provide a vehicle for the transmission of the gravitational force. And second, it might also be the medium for the spiritual forces necessary to animate an otherwise inert universe.

Newton's 'theo-physics' did go to extremes that seem simply weird to us now. He turned his science to such matters as the dimensions of Solomon's temple, the number of the Beast, and the recovery of lost knowledge from ancient times. One of his close followers identified over 300 occasions in which biblical prophecy was supported by mathematics (though he made the fatal mistake of predicting the end of the world just 30 years ahead of his own time). Scientific luminaries such as Joseph Priestley and David Hartley valued Newton's alchemy too. They routinely and favourably cited him for his expertise in esoteric matters. But one should hesitate to mock. Think instead what speculations of today will seem outlandish to scientists 300 years hence. The multi-universe theory? Eleven dimensional space? Memes?

Not that such considerations humbled others. Leibniz, a contemporary rival of Newton once joked thus: 'According to their doctrine [Newton and followers], God Almighty wants to wind up his watch from time to time: otherwise it would cease to move. He had not, it seems, sufficient foresight to make it a perpetual motion.' But Leibniz misunderstood Newton's premise. Science could not explain God away. Quite the opposite: science was a way of glimpsing the majesty of the divine. The very regularity of the world he was unveiling originates in 'the counsel and dominion of an intelligent and powerful Being', Newton wrote. This was evidence for, not against, faith: 'the Supreme God exists necessarily, and by the same necessity he exists always and everywhere'. Newton was not orthodox. He went to great lengths to conceal his disbelief in the Trinity, not least because it was against the law. However, the pressing question for him was not, does God exist, but how does God intervene in the world, and how does science fit in with a single philosophy that is both natural and divine?

In other words, his scientific work was part of a broader vocation to seek a deeper truth and, even more so, to honour God. At one level, the new science provided possible answers to the pressing questions of the day, like the wherewithal for miracles (in the form of events like cometary appearances or immaterial substances like ether). These issues seem anachronistic now, of course. But at another, more durable level, his specific religious concerns were an expression of an immensely energetic and engaged sense of wonder.

It is hard to be certain exactly how the intensely private Newton would have described this feeling himself but it is reasonable to suppose it is captured in a quotation he took from Milton's *Paradise Regained*:

> I don't know what I may seem to the world, but, as to myself, I seem to have been only like a boy playing on the sea shore, and diverting myself in now and then finding a smoother pebble or prettier shell than ordinary, whilst the great ocean of truth lay all undiscovered before me.

There is a wondering humility there - that the pebbles and shells of mathematical equations are mere reflections of a full understanding. There is the consciousness that, for all the successes of thought and experiment, human beings see only through a glass darkly. This humility before nature, coupled with the desire to understand it better, might be thought of as the high-minded benefit of ancient alchemy.

A Spirituality of Science

Many of Newton's contemporaries were into alchemy for reasons of money. They were paid to research and hoped to reap the rewards of the Midas touch. However, Newton was part of a long tradition that was critical of the merits and even the possibility of such base alchemic aims.

In 1627, Francis Bacon wrote about the 'making of gold' in his *Naturall Historie in ten Centuries*, lamenting how alchemy too often nurtures 'vanities', 'superstitions' and 'forgeries'. He preferred a more altruistic alchemy that valued experimentation for the benefits it brought to the world at large, not for its profits. A similar attitude was adopted a generation before Newton by Robert Boyle, often called the father of modern chemistry. In his book, *The Sceptical Chymist*, he laid out his loathing of the grasping obscurantism often associated with alchemy. He shows great appreciation for 'adepts' and later thought that he was close to turning quicksilver into gold. However, his call was for discipline, clarity and the full reporting of investigations.

In these more moral assessments of alchemy can be seen a concern for its spiritual, not material, significance. In general, this tradition saw alchemy as a framework in which the transformation of the alchemist was as significant an aim as the transmutation of matter. The Philosopher's Stone - the mysterious substance that is the common ingredient to all alchemic concerns - was aligned with love, a love for creation. The search for the perfect metal, gold, was taken as an allegory of the perfection of humanity. Rather like the search for the holy grail, that presumably many knew would and could never be actually found, these quests were valued for the way they took the devotee to the limits of knowledge, in a synthesis of the scientific and the spiritual. It nurtured a sense of humility by underlining the fact that there was always more to explain. It nurtured a sense of wonder by emphasising the tremendousness of the cosmos. It was expressed in esoteric terms not so much because of inherited superstitions (Newton and his fellows were not fools) but because it strove to describe what was taken as being essentially indescribable. To believe that the alchemic efforts of Newton and others were futile is to miss the point. Like the ancient oracle, whose wisdom derived from equivocal words that forced a struggle of interpretation, alchemy's allure was not to dissolve but to enter into its very mysteriousness.

ALCHEMY'S INHERITORS

Alchemy as an explicitly acknowledged goal of science died out as the scientific worldview became mainstream (in fact, lead can now be turned into gold by bombarding the metal with high energy particles - though the expense of the process far outweighs any profit from the gold). But I suspect that contemporary cosmologists embody something of the old alchemic spirit. In the cosmologist's world, objects millions of light years away are as near as the corner shop, and eons of time pass in a moment. It is they who ask the grandest questions in science. How large is the universe? How old is it? What is it made of? When will it end? They also deal in great unknowns - like dark matter, dark energy, back holes and event horizons. Moreover, there is today, in cosmology, a palpable sense that discoveries of immense importance are just around the corner, discoveries that will greatly expand our knowledge of the universe. And this focuses on one question in particular, the question of the cosmos's content.

Determining what the universe is made of matters so much because, on the scale of galaxies, Newton's mighty force rules alone. Gravity, in turn, cares only about one thing - mass. The nature of the mass that fills the void is therefore crucial. Without this piece of the puzzle, the cosmic story, from the split seconds after the big bang to the universe's final fate, remains radically incomplete. The problem is that it is hard to be sure what is out there. Matter can only be seen in space if it shines and since cosmologists now believe that perhaps 95 per cent of the universe is dark, it follows that most of the universe has never been directly observed at all. There are various candidates for this dark matter, though no-one, as yet, knows which one is right.

Alongside the search for the dark matter of the universe runs a search for another great unknown, that of dark energy. Dark energy is an otherwise unobserved force that seems to be propelling the cosmos apart. It was unwittingly foreseen by Einstein when his mathematical explorations compelled him to add an extra term to one of his equations - the so-called cosmological constant represented by a lambda. Some scientists call this dark energy 'quintessence', a field that fluctuates and fills space and time. It is important to discover more about this dark energy since it will not be possible to say for sure whether the universe will exist indefinitely until dark energy is better understood.

The current models of the universe that cosmologists work with depend on the assumption that dark matter and possibly dark energy exist. But what if neither do? As it happens, one leading cosmologist, Carlos Frenk, was my tutor when I studied physics as an undergraduate. In 1999, I returned to Durham University where he works and asked him how long it would take to discover dark matter, the issue upon which he works. Five years, was his bold estimate. Advances in terms of the details have been made since then. But over five years on, dark matter itself remains as elusive.

Frenk puts the failure down to his being too optimistic about the speed with which experiments can be conducted in astronomy. For now, at least, he believes that dark matter will still be found. About dark energy he is less sanguine. But it seems the delay has instilled something else in him too. He senses that, one way or another, cosmology, and therefore physics, is on the verge of a paradigm shift. The search for dark matter and dark energy has thrown too much up in the air, as it were. All sorts of speculations, notably about modifications to General Relativity, have been mooted in the process. They are not likely to go away whatever happens. In other words, it could be that dark matter and dark energy are as fascinating but fantastical as any of the speculations of the alchemists. It seems increasingly likely that the universe is as we see it as a result of as yet unimagined factors.

In my experience, such as it is, I have found physicists to be remarkably comfortable with such states of affairs. Unalloyed pleasure in what is pure search is very much like the old high-minded alchemy. But physicists are the inheritors of another chapter in the history of science too. At the turn of the twentieth century, physics was more triumphalist. Most physicists thought that they were in the process of putting the finishing touches to the picture of the world that originated with Newton. The mood was well captured by the German mathematician, David Hilbert. At the second International Congress of Mathematicians in Paris, in 1900, he published a list of 23 outstanding problems that he looked forward to being solved during the forthcoming century. 'What methods, what new facts will the new century reveal in the vast and rich field of mathematical thought?,' he said in his speech to the Congress.

Some of his problems were quickly solved. Others were not - not least, the challenge of putting physics on a satisfactory foundation. They remain outstanding to this day. In other words, if one can admire

Hilbert's enthusiasm, his optimism was wildly misplaced. Physics is not over. Even Stephen Hawking, the successor to Newton at Cambridge University, who once thought that a physical 'Theory of Everything' was within reach and would be tantamount to understanding the mind of God, now testifies that physics will go on forever.

These physicists have discovered something of profound significance about science. It has been reflected in developments in the philosophy of science in the 100 or more years since. The traditional view of science, as the philosopher Hilary Putnam calls it, has been challenged by more dynamic accounts.

PARADIGM SHIFTS

The traditional view is that scientific knowledge is cumulative. Like doing a jigsaw, that may take time and involve taking pieces out as well as putting them in place, the traditional view was that science is the process of assembling a picture of the world that will one day be complete. Such a marvellous achievement was thought possible because of the scientific method. The scientific method rests on induction. Scientists collate sets of empirically verifiable premises from which a conclusion, that is more than could have been anticipated from any one of the premises, can be induced. For example: the sun rises one day, and then the next, and then the next, from which it is concluded that the sun will rise every day.

The trouble is that the history of physics over the last 100 years has not looked anything like this cumulative idea of scientific discovery. In the generation after Hilbert and his contemporaries, Einstein published his theories of relativity and quantum mechanics was born. Physics was revolutionised, and today arguably awaits revolution again. This has caused philosophers of science to question the traditional view.

Various alternatives have been offered. Thomas Kuhn thought that the apparently cumulative periods of scientific endeavour were only one part of the story. He called this normal science, when scientists pursue their line of research on the assumption that it fits into the great puzzle of knowledge that awaits completion. However, there is another part of the story, when science undergoes a paradigm shift. As the uncertainties of one paradigm become irresistible, scientists fight it out to establish a new one. When that has happened, a new round of normal science is initiated and the illusion of cumulative truth returns. This is arguably what happened to physics at the 1920s. Scientists then thought that they were just putting the finishing touches to the picture of the world that originated with Newton, were it not for a handful of experiments that kept throwing a spanner in the works. These experiments confounded the wave theory of light by showing how light could behave as if it were particles of energy too. Some took this conundrum to be a result of errors; they took the 'flawed' experiments to be addressing the wrong questions. However, eventually, the weight of evidence became unavoidable. From what seemed a mere glitch, a whole new paradigm in science was born, namely, the indeterminate, probabilistic world of quantum mechanics.

Kuhn's alternative model of science is the one most widely accepted by those who reject the traditional one. His normal science looks very much like the industrial processes under which science is carried out in commerce and universities. However, Kuhn's model also entails that social forces play a part in the determination of 'scientific' truth too, when science is undergoing a paradigm shift. Which is to say that science is not wholly scientific. In questioning the traditional model of science, an ambiguity as to the veracity of science has crept in. Science is neither seamlessly cumulative nor can it wholly account for the processes through which its results are derived.

A different model of science was proposed by Karl Popper. He rejected the method of induction, following David Hume who argued that it was no more reliable than a belief. Thinking of the rising sun again, Hume pointed out that just because it rose yesterday and today is no proof that it will rise tomorrow, for all that it seems very likely. Popper thought that induction was more like a process of informed guesswork. The way science works, he argued, is that scientists come up with hypotheses based on their intuition. They then test them by observation. These tests do not verify the hypothesis, as the traditional view of science would have them do. Rather, all they can do is show that the hypothesis is not false. So, the best scientific theories are the ones that are most easily falsifiable for, if they stand up, they are more likely to be right.

However, in offering this model of science, Popper also implied that science is never true, though it may come asymptotically close. (In practice, because the best falsifiable theories depend on the quality of the method used to test them, which is also hard to get right, scientific theories will routinely be overthrown by other ones.) Which is also to say, to deploy another piece of philosophical language, that science cannot adopt a correspondence theory of truth for itself.

Kuhn and Popper are both philosophical heirs of Immanuel Kant. He famously pointed out that our image of the world around us could not be a mirror image of things as they are in themselves because the human mind imposes its own structures of thought onto the world. It cannot do otherwise, for without our own concepts of things we would not be able to understand anything. As Putnam puts it: 'Scientific theories are not simply dictated to us by the facts.' The wave/particle duality of light is a good case in point. When viewed using one set of theoretical spectacles, light looks like a wave. When using another, it looks like particles. So, there are various ways that a scientist can use to describe facts - what philosophers call equivalent descriptions. All in all, be it by paradigm shifts or discarding falsified theories, it might be said that science evolves by rejecting ideas when shown wrong and by taking as much account as possible of the interaction between these theories and the human conventions within which they arose. However, it can never be absolutely right.

This philosophy of science - what it is, how it works and what it achieves - is passionately contested by philosophers and those scientists who are interested in it. What began in the twentieth century and continues into the twenty-first is nothing less than a 'struggle for the soul of science', as the sociologist Steve Fuller has described it in the title of a book. It is a battle that is set to continue. However, it seems safe to say that science can never again think of itself as simply incorrigible. A kernel of uncertainty has been found at the centre of the scientific worldview. Science is, to one degree or another, an agnostic enterprise.

WORKING WITH MYSTERIES

Such uncertainty might be taken as a counsel of despair - as if science's mission to explain things were ultimately doomed to failure. However, with cosmologists at least, the mystery of the universe is, in fact, a powerful motivating factor. For them, the wonder it nurtures lies at the heart of the scientific project: an inherent inability to answer all the questions is the very thing that drives it. The question that hangs over contemporary cosmology is the direct result of this. Are dark mass and dark energy to physics today what photons were to physics 100 years ago? One might even go a step further: what new mystery will do the same thing in 100 years time? Again, one detects echoes of old alchemy.

It might be tempting to say that cosmology is overblown or, conversely, to conclude that science is radically unintelligible. Terms like dark energy might be taken as hermetic ciphers (that some versions of the theory talk of dark energy as 'phantom energy' and 'quintessence' compounds that sense). This would make modern cosmology out to be hardly more scientific than, say, the Egyptian *Book of the Dead*. That is not right. Certainly, there are echoes of the old interest in ethers in the talk of dark matter and dark energy. But that is not to dismiss it. It is important to remember two things. First, the words used to describe modern cosmology are actually analogies that convey essentially mathematical entities. The parallel to drawn on here is the fore-mentioned dual nature of light. Though it is strictly speaking impossible to say that light is both a particle and a wave, the inconsistency disappears at the mathematical level. As Werner Heisenberg only slightly too unequivocally put it, in his book *Physics and Philosophy*, 'When this vague and unsystematic use of language leads us into difficulties, the physicist has to withdraw into the mathematical scheme and its unambiguous correlation with experimental facts.' However, and secondly, this points to the deeper problem - the one highlighted by Kant. For all the predictive success of equations, and their ability to handle apparent paradoxes, the gap between the world as mathematics encapsulates it and the world as it is in itself, whatever that might be, still remains unbridged. So perhaps to the layman and physicist alike, strange terms like dark matter or energy are valuable reminders that what is being discussed at the frontiers of science is both contentious and, like action at a distance, essentially not at all well understood. If they convey an air of mystery then, in an importance sense, that is good.

I should be clear about this: by using the word mystery, let alone talking about alchemic parallels in cosmology, I do not mean to invoke some sense of the supernatural. Rather, it is to highlight what might be

called 'natural mystery'. Natural mysteries need to be distinguished
from natural problems that scientific techniques will, in time, unravel.
The former are genuinely mysterious phenomenon, in the sense that,
although they occur in the natural realm, their fundamental nature is not
amenable to scientific inspection. Sometimes, something that was once
a mystery may become a problem that is then solved. However, at the
limits of current cosmological understanding, for example, there appears
to be something that is fundamentally mysterious.

I suspect that this, or some version of it, will always remain. Consider
again the force central to cosmology, namely, gravity. When Newton discovered the inverse square law, which describes how gravity works, he
did not for a minute think that he had shown what gravity is. It is, if you
think about it, quite magical that the Moon should stay in orbit around
the Earth, and the Earth around the Sun, for all that they do so in
entirely predictable ways. Newton thought that it was the power of
God, revealed in an immaterial force, that lay behind his formulae.

Einstein improved the description. His Theory of General Relativity
shows gravity as a distortion in the space/time continuum - whence the
pictorial analogy of heavenly bodies moving along the contours of gravitational depressions, like floating balls swinging by celestial whirlpools.
But whilst this description predicts certain phenomenon that Newton
could not, like gravitational waves (whose detection, incidentally, is
another one of the great goals of contemporary physics), in terms of
actually understanding what gravity is, it only pushes the mystery back
a step. What, after all, does the analogy of the space/time continuum
represent of the universe as it is in itself?

Another example of a natural mystery is the nature of time. The nub
of the problem here is that physics understands time in a way that is
incompatible with the way we experience it. Time in physical equations
is a variable, t, that can increase ('move into the future'), remain the
same ('stand still'), or decrease ('travel into the past'). This leads to
many paradoxes. Maxwell's Equations, for example, that otherwise
describe electromagnetic radiation very brilliantly, operate in a world in
which a radio wave can be received before it has been sent. Alternatively,
the equations of quantum mechanics are quite at ease with particles that
can move back in time, as well as forward.

Illus. 2.2:   Cosmologists have always been humbled by the vastness of the things that they study.

What is missing is time's steady progress at one second per second, the irresistible quality that is its very essence as far as our experience is concerned. Various theories have been proposed to account for this 'arrow of time'. The second law of thermodynamics is one: time moves forward in the same way that energy tends to an equilibrium. But just how the two phenomena might connect is unclear, as is why the second law should dictate that time changes at a steady rate (within any particular inertial frame) - which entropy need not.

These mysteries within physics not only produce a relaxed attitude towards uncertainties in cosmologists but also a marked humility. An example of this is found in the work of the Astronomer Royal, Martin Rees. His latest book is entitled *Our Final Century? Will the Human Race Survive the 21st Century?*. Alternatively, he recently presented a TV series called *What We Still Don't Know*. It is very striking that such a distinguished scientist should adopt such apocalyptic and agnostic tones. Rees's apocalyptic mood is the result of an explicitly humble perspective that stems directly from his astronomical interests. The immensity of the universe that he studies leads him to show a notable reserve, even diffidence, when it comes to celebrating the successes of science as a whole. For example, he is very conscious that the Earth may well have more time ahead of it than the time that lies behind it, and who knows what might evolve in the eons that stretch into the cosmological future? Alternatively, he makes the point that perhaps even in a relatively short time what people call scientific progress now may come to be seen as a regress - something that is not hard to imagine given the environmental disaster that may be only around the corner. Put at its most general level, there are all sorts of unknowns in the future, and, conscious of the agnosticism that entails, Rees is typical of the humble breed of scientist.

HUMILITY AND HUBRIS

Now, the savvy reader will have noticed by now that in this chapter, entitled 'Cosmologists and Darwinists', only one breed of scientist has been mentioned. They may be asking why the other has not. Well, yes. And it is now time to turn to it - though with what is undoubtedly a gross generalisation. My excuse for making this generalisation is that whilst there are undoubtedly exceptions - indeed, at least one biologist has made the observation I am about to make - there is philosophical value in making it. That is that if physics, typified by the cosmologists, tends to be characterised by a certain humility, then biology, typified by the Darwinists, appears coloured by hubris.

A succinct example is provided in a short essay written by the increasingly infamous Richard Dawkins. It appears in Ben Rogers's book *Is Nothing Sacred?*. The book grapples with the thorny issue of whether the scientific worldview undermines the sense in which some things - whether it be a glorious vista, a work of art, or human life itself - might be called sacred. Dawkins takes the opportunity to underline that certain experiences do provoke feelings of awe in him, and that they might even be taken by some for a kind of religious experience. He prefers to put it down to a poetic imagination which, in turn, he sees as a manifestation of human nature.

Now, there is nothing necessarily hubristic in that point of view as it stands. However, Dawkins reveals his colours in the last paragraph of his piece. He writes: 'As scientists, and biological scientists, it's up to us to explain [feelings of awe], and I expect that one day we shall.' In this conclusion, he does not doubt that such a biological explanation is possible, or even that it could be partial. Neither is there any acknowledgement of insights into the sacred from other spheres of human knowledge, be it in the poetry of a man like Coleridge or the philosophy of a man like Kant. According to Dawkins, all explanations of sacredness are or will be subsumed within the meta-narrative of Darwinian biology.

How can this ideological overconfidence be understood? Perhaps Dawkins was just being careless in his essay - though the way he routinely encourages accusations of hubris in his work leads one to suspect that, if he was overstating his case, it is done so deliberately. Another possibility is offered by Robert Winston, the fertility expert. He has written a book called *The Story of God*. The book has irritated religious reviewers since it presents an eccentric view of belief - focussed more on weeping statues than serious theology. However, apart from the fact that it is written by a biologist who is happy to confess to being a practising Jew, he also concurs with the observation that biologists are notably more confident about their science than physicists. He puts the difference down to the former thinking that they have it 'all wrapped up' - the very thing that the modern cosmologist is so conscious of not having done. But biologists don't have it wrapped up, Winston retorts. Even within the limits of their own fields, there is still a long way to go. The suggestion is that biology, particularly in its more youthful neo-Darwinian guise, suffers from an amnesia when it comes to the history of science. It forgets that physics has been here before and had to undergo a process of reassessing itself as a result.

Having said that, biology can perhaps be forgiven to a degree. For a new factor undoubtedly reinforces its assertiveness. Many biologists, and certainly individuals like Dawkins, perceive that they are in a pitched battle against creationism - the conservative Christian conviction, dressed up as science, that denies evolution and says the world was created by God in seven days. The unfortunate thing is that this often forces them into an equal and opposite extreme: the strategy seems to be to extend the reach of Darwinism to so many spheres of life that it leaves the creationists with no toeholds. No doubt some Darwinists are conviction atheists and are quite happy with the extremity of their position. That they dominate the discussion is, though, a shame because all it achieves is a fanning of fundamentalist flames. Attention to light, rather than heat, might be more helpful. It might reveal that at the grassroots level the objection amongst conservative Christians is more to Darwinism as an ideology than a scientific theory. Sure, many middle American mums and dads might confess belief in the seven days of creation or a few thousand years as the age of the universe. But these beliefs are expressions of a deeper worry about what they perceive as the moral nihilism that comes with Darwinian ideology.

The same concerns are also behind the movement called Intelligent Design. Intelligent Design is the belief that the universe exhibits features that can be shown to be the result of a deliberate agency. It is, again, pitched as an alternative to Darwinism - another mistake since it is not a science. Rather, it co-opts the description of the world provided by science and adds a supernatural layer which is taken as the fundamental cause of natural processes. (In this way, it is different from the so-called proof for the existence of God from design. For Thomas Aquinas, its chief proponent, the point was not to portray God as 'hands on' in the universe. Rather it was to say that, whatever physical processes might be observed, the universe has a purpose that finds its ultimate fulfilment in God.)

But if Intelligent Design is wrong to pose as science, it is right inasmuch as it too reflects the way that Darwinian thought often becomes ideological and insists on overreaching itself. Not only does Darwinism have a tendency to think of itself as incorrigible, the mistake that the physicists have learnt to avoid, but it also has a tendency to think that its description of biological processes either can or will be able to explain everything that 'right-thinking' human beings might choose to study. This is the belief that science can completely usurp the role that religion has played as a source of meaning. It is the thought that science will explain all things that it deems to matter and dismiss everything else as superstition. It is the ideology known as scientism.

VISIONS OF REALITY: SCIENCE AND WONDER

> We feel that even when all possible scientific questions have been
> answered, the problems of life have not been put to rest.
>
> Wittgenstein

DARWINISM'S HOPES FOR ITS SCIENCE are not new. Way back in
ancient Athens a not-dissimilar optimism was in the air. The philosophers now called the pre-Socratic natural philosophers were widely
known for their investigations of the world (it was from some of them
that ancient atheism arose). And they had good reason to be wowed by
their science's achievements. For example, its amazing power was being
made manifest in the construction of the Parthenon - a technological
wonder that has inspired awe for 2500 years.

One should not underestimate the remarkably prescient nature of
their discoveries too. Parmenides realised that the moon reflects the
light of the sun. Democritus postulated the basic units of nature as
atoms existing in a void. Pythagoras, as well as his celebrated theorem,
worked out that day and night were far better explained by the earth
going round the sun, not vice versa. Empedocles argued that the natural
world was made up of elements, and although he considered that there
were only four (earth, fire, air and water), he was right in presuming
that the material world could be explained by a continual flux of
elemental integration and disintegration.

These searching minds also anticipated many of the philosophical
problems with which science wrestles to this day. Democritus, for example, knew that whilst there was power in his postulate that atoms formed

Illus. 3.1:   The Parthenon has made the wonder of technology manifest for 2500 years.

matter and that matter, in turn, formed the world as we experience it, his atomic theory was also limited as an explanation: at the atomic level it can account for the material world around us, but it cannot account for itself, because that, in turn, would require an explanation involving particles smaller than atoms to account for atoms. This search for ever smaller, more elusive forces and particles is one that quantum theory is still caught up in to this day. The problem is that particle physics - ancient or modern - begs the question of what accounts for its fundamentals.

A different perennial problem was anticipated by Parmenides. What survives of his work includes two explanations of the world, called the *Way of Truth* and the *Way of Seeing* (titles that on the face of it chime remarkably with the thought of Kant). The *Way of Seeing* includes his astronomical achievements and simultaneously throws them into question: how do we know, he implies, that the way we divide the world up, as any reductionist science must do, actually reflects the world as it is? Are the divisions purely arbitrary or would a true map of reality show similar divisions? Put in a modern idiom, is the universe truly mathematical (is *pi* in the sky?, it is sometimes asked) or is mathematics just very successful at describing certain aspects of it? In other words, Parmenides understood that science needs theories in order to interpret observations, but whether these theories correspond with reality is not something that science can itself answer.

Another speculation with a contemporary ring can be heard in the thoughts of Empedocles. He felt that the integrating and disintegrating cycles of the elements implied the need for a moral interpretation alongside the physical. After all, is it not as if the universe is moving from harmony to discord, and then back again, and perhaps according to some fundamental forces - he called them Strife and Friendship - he asked?

A twofold tale I shall tell: at one time it grew to be one alone out of many, at another again it grew apart to be many out of one. Double is the birth of mortal things and double their failing; for one is brought to birth and destroyed by the coming together of all things, the other is nurtured and flies apart as they grow apart again. And these things never cease their continual exchange, now through Friendship all coming together into one, now again each carried apart by the hatred of Strife.

It came quite naturally for him to slip from the realm of scientific theory into the realm of moral speculation. But then, in the following genera-tion, the bubble of confidence was burst when this growing faith in science was challenged - by none other than Socrates.

CAUSES AND CONDITIONS

Plato preserved Socrates' challenge to the proto-scientism of his times in his dialogue the *Phaedo*. Phaedo was an intimate of Socrates. In Plato's dialogue, he recalls the last conversation Socrates had with his friends - a poignant time to reflect on the nature of things. In these hours, Socrates pondered the significance of life and death, and how one might rejoice in the former and prepare for the latter. And he recalled his first forays in the world of ideas. 'When I was a young man I was wonderfully keen on that wisdom which they call natural science, for I thought it splendid to know the causes of everything, why it comes to be, why it perishes and why it exists,' he recollects. He sought answers to questions remarkably similar to those asked by modern Darwinists: what matter is it that allows us to think? Is it our brains that hear, see and smell? And when our brains perish, do our memories and insights perish too?

At first, he thought that science was a good way of asking such ques-tions because, as it claimed, it did indeed seem to explain things and causes. However, his optimism did not last. For, upon further inspec-tion, the explanations it offered seemed really quite easy to unravel. Socrates offers a simple example in Plato's dialogue: whether $1 + 1 = 2$. There are good reasons to doubt it. For one thing, there are examples in nature when $1 + 1 \neq 2$, as when two raindrops coalesce. Alternatively, there is, strictly speaking, no mathematic proof that $1 + 1 = 2$. Today, mathematicians would say that it is, rather, something that follows from the definition of natural numbers $(1, 2, 3, 4 \dots)$.

Such technicalities might be thought trivial, perhaps because we intu-itively know when $1 + 1 = 2$ and when it does not. Alternatively - and as modern philosophers have argued in response to Hume's observation that science rests upon inferences which are, essentially, a form of belief - the value of science is that it produces the best explanations of things or the ones that are most likely (as Dawkins once observed, when flying in a jumbo it is quite clear which explanation of flying you trust).

However, the complications associated with scientific explanations become more marked when one moves to aspects of life that might inform human meaning. The ambiguity of science, which may or may not matter when it comes to describing things, most certainly does matter when it comes to human beings. In fact, not only do scientific explanations of human behaviour now seem increasingly incomplete but, humanly speaking, they become increasingly irrelevant.

This all became clear to Socrates when he read another pre-Socratic natural philosopher, Anaxagoras. Anaxagoras followed an atomic theory of matter, similar to that of Democritus. However, he realised that although atomic processes might more or less explain how matter can appear in so many forms in the inanimate world, its weakness becomes increasingly pronounced when it comes to the living. His point is that living things do not behave like inanimate matter. Plants, for example, grow. Animals show intention. And when it comes to humans, physical causes are almost neither here nor there. With people, desires, conscious and unconscious, are the 'causes' that count. To put it another way, and recall a subsequent distinction made by Aristotle: human beings want not just to exist, but to live and live well. So even when doing 'animal' things, we loathe living like animals: we prefer, say, to eat tasty food, not just muck; to sleep in a comfortable bed, not just on the floor; and to make love, not merely copulate. So, Anaxagoras postulated an all-controlling force that he called Mind - 'the finest of all things and the purest, and it possesses all knowledge about everything, and it has the greatest strength.' This, he thought, is what lies behind the world, and that we see particularly in those living phenomenon that demonstrate volition. It might seem a superstitious, unscientific belief to us. But it had the advantage, Socrates thought, of implying that the world was ordered in the best possible way - a principle of economy, simplicity and beauty that, if in a disenchanted form, is in fact still compelling to scientists today.

The problem Socrates had with it, though, was that for all its aesthetic appeal it actually explained nothing. For example, Socrates asks himself, again in Plato's dialogue, why he is sitting in the prison with his friends awaiting death. Following Anaxagoras, he might say it is due to his mind and the way it controls his body. However, this seems a somewhat reductive assessment of the situation. It would say, Socrates continued:

> I am sitting here because my body consists of bones and sinews, because the bones are hard and are separated by joints, that the sinews are such as to contract and relax, that they surround the bones along with flesh and skin which hold them together, then as the bones are hanging in their sockets, the relaxation and contraction of the sinews enable me to bend my limbs, and that is the cause of my sitting here with my limbs bent.

As might be suspected from this shaggy dog story of an explanation, Socrates thinks it foolish (one can imagine the modern equivalent of neurons, synapses and nerves firing). Science fails to explain his sitting in another sense too. If the body's chief aim is survival, as might seem reasonable from a scientific point of view, then it would suggest that Socrates should have escaped prison. According to the scientific worldview, his sinews and bones should have been miles away.

So why am I sat here, he asks again? The answer is only very remotely to do with his body or mind. It is actually because the Athenians have condemned him to death. Moreover, Socrates could have escaped and lived. But he has decided it is right to stay and die. In other words, Socrates is in prison for a reason that science does not begin to get a handle on. The 'cause' of his predicament is a moral one.

Socrates continues, speculating that someone might retort, well that may be true, but, at a basic level, you could not be sitting in prison without your sinews and bones having moved in certain ways. That is right, Socrates admits: 'But surely to say that they are the cause of what I do, and not that I have chosen the moral course, is to speak very lazily and carelessly.' A much better way of putting it is to say that it is a *condition* of his sitting that he has sinews and bones, but not a cause. That they don't, he suggests, is the mistake scientists make when they present their explanations of nature as causes of human behaviour. They fool themselves and 'grope around in the dark' by confusing moral causes with physical conditions.

So Socrates became disillusioned with science. When it came to matters of moral significance, it was just not asking the right questions nor using the right tools. He diagnosed that it is the dogmatic prioritisation of scientific conditions over moral causes, when a moral explanation is more appropriate, that leads the scientific worldview to overreach itself. He decided that he must turn away from science. He did not want science to stop. But he saw that if it is meaning that interests you, then it is moral philosophy you must study. In effect, what Socrates had done was add another category of knowledge to which science has no access. The domain in which the latter works well is that of natural problems. When it comes to natural mysteries - like the nature of gravity and time - it starts to come unstuck. And when it comes to things like moral causes, it may be able to contribute a few minor conditions, but they are not only far from sufficient but, without philosophy, they are simply blind.

POLICIES FOR HAPPINESS

Not everyone engaged in modern Darwinism is a follower of such scientism, of course. Neither were all the natural philosophers of Socrates' day atheists. However, in both cultures one can see that a shift is taking place, to a dominant scientific worldview. This tends to encourage a lesser, more prevalent version of scientism, sometimes called naturalism. Whilst appreciating that full-blown scientism is overblown, naturalism places great store on science, saying that it overshadows other forms of knowledge as a way to certainty and truth. Socrates' challenge was aimed at naturalism as much as scientism and is still pertinent today.

This is not just an ideological battle. It profoundly shapes the way we now live. Consider as an example some of the hopes and expectations people have for contemporary neuroscience. Anyone who reads a newspaper will be familiar with stories about brain scans revealing the secrets of anything from consciousness to altruism, often reported as if no-one before had anything much to say on the subject. Wild headlines are often misleading, of course (as headlines about genes being discovered for this or that are too). However, there is more substantial evidence that the philosophical mistake of the pre-Socratic scientists is being made again.

Consider the neuroscience of happiness. The scientific breakthrough that led to this subdivision of the discipline was the identification of regions in the brain that are associated with good and bad feeling. According to this work, there is a part of the left frontal lobe that fires when good feelings are experienced and a part of the right frontal lobe that fires when bad feelings arise. The result has been interpreted by some as of key interest not only to brain scientists but to moral philosophers too because it provides an objective indicator of what people are feeling. This, they say, is needed to overcome the scepticism that derives from certain philosophical traditions that doubt it is possible to know what another person is feeling (because I can only observe you, and not see into your brain, and from that only infer what you are experiencing). The hope is that because individuals can be wired up and monitored as, say, they laugh or cry, confidence can return to interpreting the meaning of tears: if the left brain lights up, they are indeed tears of joy; if the right brain lights up, they are tears of sadness.

This science has been taken out of the laboratory and into government. Its advocates say that it provides firm foundations for social policies that aim to promote the ways in which people can live more happily. Richard Layard has explained how in his book, *Happiness: Lessons from a New Science*. He argues that as a result of philosophical scepticism, policymakers had lost confidence in the idea of Jeremy Bentham that a good society is one in which happiness is maximised for the greatest number of people. They had worried that they could not say for sure what it was for people to be truly happy. For this reason politicians in recent years have focussed on things like maximising people's rights or opportunities - legal entities that are tangible in ways that the pursuit of happiness is not. But, says Layard, happiness can be put back on the agenda as a goal of government because it can now be measured: happiness is made tangible by 'solid psychology and neuroscience', he says.

One cannot question the frustration that lies behind Layard's hope. Why, he asks, have human beings in the West become no happier over the last 50 years, a period that has seen unparalleled economic growth? He also rightly laments the limitations inherent in politics based mostly upon rights and opportunity. They are endlessly contested and make people highly individualistic. This is why he wants neuroscience to 'vindicate' Bentham's approach to politics.

But does it? Let us develop the distinction that Aristotle derived from Socrates' experience, the distinction between merely existing and living well. It was based upon two uses of the word 'life' (he was helped by the fact that in Greek there are two words for life - *zoē* and *bios*). Aristotle noticed that there is animal-like life (*zoē*), that is life as in being healthy, fed and housed - what could be called 'zoological' existing. And there is social-like life (*bios*), that is life as in not merely living as animals do but living well as human beings aspire to. *Bios* includes such aspects as being happy, as well as, say, being fulfilled, educated, inspired and having purpose. The distinction is useful because science is an excellent promoter of life in the zoological sense: technologies from science have clearly made countless humans healthier, better fed and housed. But science is blind when it comes to the moral matter of not merely existing but living well.

The confusion implicit in the revival of the politics of happiness is, then, that the science upon which it is based operates in the realm of *zoē*, whilst happiness is mostly about *bios*. For example, whilst neuroscience can watch a brain firing it cannot ask the question of what a 'good feeling' itself might be. The main problem here is that feelings are subjective experiences whereas the science operates at the level of objective activity. Even if it is assumed that there is a relatively straightforward correlation between what someone is feeling and what their brain is doing, there are important philosophical questions to ask. For example, is not pleasure very different from contentment which is again very different from joyfulness which is similarly different from happiness - and yet all would be called good feelings? And underneath all that lies the fundamental question of what happiness is? Today it is generally taken to mean a peak or sustained experience of positive feeling. A quintessential example might be the sensation an athlete has when they have won a race. However, Aristotle convincingly argued that this notion is inadequate. He said that a happy person is one who is good, in two senses. First, they are good at what they do. And second, they are good because of the person they become in doing it. In short, happiness comes to a life lived with an overall good purpose. This explains his otherwise rather puzzling maxim that a person cannot tell whether they were truly happy until they die: happiness is a reflection of the shape of a life as a whole not a measure of isolated or even extended moments in it.

Susan Greenfield, head of the Royal Institution, has made the general point. It is easy to be beguiled by the technology behind neuroscience, she has said. Brain scans, after all, are amazing. But one should not forget that the answers technology provides are only as good as the questions that are asked of it.

METAPHORICAL SCIENCE

The mathematician Michael Atiyah, sometime Master of Trinity College, Cambridge, and President of the Royal Society, is another scientist who has deployed a particularly powerful comparison to highlight the way scientific accounts of things come to replace the effort to truly understand the full nature of the matter at hand. He calls it a Faustian pact.

> The devil says: 'I will give you this powerful machine, and it will answer any question you like. All you need to do is give me your soul: give up something and you will have this marvellous machine.'

Of course, the scientific machine thinks that it can cheat the devil by remembering that the measurements and formulae it deals in are abstracted from the nature of things and the experiences of people. But because the answers that science provides are so compelling, so complete in themselves, it is too easy to forget that and slip into thinking that they are themselves complete.

Science is subject to these sleights of hands in other ways too. What I am thinking of here are the metaphors that are used to animate scientific accounts of phenomena. To be fair to the biologists, cosmology is prone to this too. Consider, the standard model of the Big Bang. The physicist Brian Ridley shows how what is actually Judaeo-Christian imagery is used to add cólour to the story of the Big Bang in his book *On Science*:

> In the beginning was perfect symmetry at enormously high energies where everything was like everything else (that is, if we could

speak of a beginning, which we cannot because time is mixed with space because of gravity). The subsequent evolution of the universe broke the symmetry (as it does in the Book of Genesis with the creation of Adam and Eve) and the various families of particles with their interactions became distinct (Fall from Grace). A new story of creation is being formed, but how much is science and how much myth remains to be seen.

Alternatively, there is the way biologists talk about DNA. The four nucleotides of DNA are represented by letters AGCT. They arrange themselves in what are called codons. These, in turn, are taken to be the words of the genetic instructions for the cell. Now, clearly an organism like a human being, consisting of trillions of cells, is going to be a fantastically complicated product of the DNA double helix, mixed up with even more subtle intercellular and environmental factors (to say nothing of the psychosomatic). But DNA's descriptive similarity to a code, coupled to a technological age's trust in data, inevitably leads to the assumption that DNA is not only the determining factor in life - the notion captured in Dawkins's metaphor 'the selfish gene' - but is nothing less than the 'code of life'. The insertion of non-scientific imagery does not stop here, for the idea that human beings are information-processing machines does not account for everything that is claimed for DNA. Again, religious metaphors are needed for that. For example, the idea that to read DNA is to understand life is a Protestant trope - DNA as the 'Book of Life' or the Bible. Alternatively, when coupled to genetic determinism, DNA comes to look very much like the immortal soul: it embodies in nucleotides an essence of life that survives the death of the body by being passed on, incorporeally, from generation to generation.

It is possible to argue that these metaphors are passive: when deployed, they are used as analogies, serving to popularise science, as opposed to informing hard-core research. However, these metaphors are powerful for a reason. They feed the illusion that science can provide a complete worldview. On the vision that drives modern cosmology, Ridley continues his expose of the story of the Big Bang by parodying the imperative to find simplicity at the original of the present, chaotic universe:

> Now, this devilish plethora of fermions and bosons is not to be
> borne. Surely, this state of affairs is the result of a Fall. Surely,
> there was once an Eden where fermions and bosons were merely
> potentialities within a perfect God particle, the Theon. Surely, the
> Big Bang was when the Theon exhibited its glory and created the
> world. And is it not the reverent and awesome duty of the sons
> and daughters of Theon to use their Theon-given rationality to
> trace their evolution back to the Godhead?

Alternatively, the idea that DNA is a code was an important motivating
factor in the billions spent on the Human Genome Project: its whole
premise was that one must be able to read the 'whole book' in order to
understand its content properly. The project will surely yield great
results but whether it will live up to its original billing, which was
nothing short of a transhuman utopia, is already being doubted.

DIMINISHING HUMANITY

Mary Midgley has done much to unpick how and where the overextended
scientific worldview goes wrong. She believes that human beings simply
cannot understand the world without resorting to myths or visions: not to
do so would be as plausible as claiming to enjoy a life that had absolutely
no meaning or value. So the question is how conscious, and therefore critical, someone is of the myths or visions they are deploying. 'If we ignore
them, we travel blindly inside myths and visions which are largely provided
by other people. This makes it much harder to know where we are going,'
she writes in *Science as Salvation: a Modern Myth and Its Meaning*. In relation
to DNA, for example, the fear is that a more-or-less unreflective assumption that 'DNA is life' might blind all kinds of genetic experimentation to
adverse outcomes, physical and moral, simply because it does not have the
resources to engage with what it is doing in a meaningful way.

The advantage that a more reflective worldview has is that it places
centre stage the fact that human beings are often ignorant. Recalling
Socrates' central conviction, it recognises that although we are higher
than the beasts of the field, we are also less than gods - the thing that

scientism and even naturalism finds hard to admit. Religion, though, at its best, provides a framework within which to negotiate the human predicament. Socratic philosophy, as we have seen and as we will develop, offers related checks and balances. Both stress the need to undergo some kind of profound reflection to highlight inherent limits. An all-powerful scientific worldview minimises this element by seeing in science a way of transcending limits altogether.

The fantasy of a science that makes humans divine is also ancient. It began with the Tower of Babel, the primordial exploitation of 'brick science' to reach heaven. A high-profile modern version of the same hubris came when Yuri Gagarin first orbited the Earth: he claimed a triumphant conquest of at least the lower heavens for humankind, saying, 'I don't see any God up here.' Since then, the fantasy seems to have become particularly intense. Perhaps this is because modern technology puts within our power not only the ability to manipulate the world around us but, with genetics, our very selves too.

> The pervading technologism leads us to think that we are on the brink of a great leap forward that will cause us to 'mutate'. It would become so easy then (and nearly 'automatic') to make objection to every reference to humanity, its weaknesses as well as its merits: 'All of that is overcome! We are in a new era! An entirely different race is born!'

So wrote the philosopher Dominique Janicaud in his book, *On the Human Condition*. His aim was not to knock the science but to point out the dangers of being led by apocalyptic talk of an 'automatic' posthuman future, nourished by a myth of overcoming limits. The fear is that the naivety that can exist in the scientific worldview's unacknowledged religiosity leads us into a future that, far from making us gods, actually diminishes our humanity.

So where is the agnostic stance in all this? What attitude might someone have who is uneasy about the utopianism peddled as our inevitable technological future, but is not simply Luddite about the achievements of science to date? How might the philosophical critique of science and its limits be translated into a more cautious but still scientifically committed culture?

CRITICAL WONDERMENT

The word 'wonderment' is found more in literature than common parlance. But its unusualness serves to emphasise qualities of marvelling, surprise and awe - perhaps tinged with fear. Wonder may or may not be explicitly linked to a religious sensibility and it does not necessarily spring from a belief in God: it is not dependent upon theological categories, though a religious imagination would appear to be particularly open to it. It stems from a profound realisation of the limits of human knowledge - our 'in-between' status in creation - that, in turn, fires a capacity for inquisitive fascination. Wonderment is what I would like to suggest as the agnostic attitude to science.

Wonderment as a response to nature is most famously found in the romantic poets. Coleridge, who suffered a crisis of belief until he came to the conclusion that both scientific and religious knowledge rested on equally uncertain grounds, provides an obvious example. One of his sonnets, *Life*, describes a melancholy country walk that is suddenly transformed when he is struck by 'the glorious prospect' all round him. With that epiphany, the woods, the meadows and the hills lift him out of his sad state and come to ravish and delight him.

A darker aspect of wonderment is suggested by the awful obsession that grips Ishmael in *Moby Dick*. He compulsively deploys every science known to humanity to try to understand the famous whale. They all fail in one way or another, and his wonder, unabated, turns into a kind of terror. It focusses on things in nature that are white. Polar bears, sharks and stallions fill one category of fearful things because they are dangerous. Whales and albatrosses occupy another: they are fearful because they are so irreducibly mysterious. 'Bethink thee of the albatross, whence come those clouds of spiritual wonderment and pale dread, in which that white phantom sails in all imaginations? Not Coleridge first threw that spell; but God's great, unflattering laureate, Nature,' Melville writes.

Luckily, nature's wonder rarely turns people mad. More common is the feeling of awesomeness that leaves one simply open mouthed. A cosmologist-like wonder adds another dimension. As well as an appreciation, it is also a desire to search, to consider and to analyse. If it awakens a reverence towards nature, it also provokes the desire to understand it. This dimension is, in fact, also reflected in Coleridge's sonnet. The epiphany that saves him does not stop with uplifting feeling; he resolves to study nature: 'New scenes of Wisdom may each step display, / And Knowledge open as my days advance!'.

So, in order to expand on the notion, consider three different aspects of agnostic wonderment that I would like to suggest might rebalance the scientific worldview, without simply rejecting it. First, the sense it gives that there is intrinsic value in nature. Second, the way it connects this scientific knowledge of the world to other forms of knowledge that of itself it cannot grasp. Third, the attitude of piety it inculcates as a result of its consciousness that there is a point at which scientific explanations stop in the face of nature's givenness. The hope is that a rich sense of scientific wonder might integrate the limitations and the value of the scientific enterprise in a single sensibility. Nurturing such a culture of agnosticism towards science, wonderment may also suggest a framework from which a fresh perspective on the moral issues that hang over contemporary science and technology could be gained.

First, then, the way in which wonderment highlights the intrinsic value in nature. It will come as no surprise to learn that philosophers express all sorts of reservations when it comes to the idea that something can have intrinsic value. For many it just sounds too much like pre-Enlightenment theism. However, there is milage in the term when intrinsic simply means the opposite of instrumental. This is the important sense of intrinsic in relation to the value of nature, since science and technology can easily proceed as if the world exists solely for human beings to exploit. The looming environmental crisis of global warming is the obvious example of such instrumentalism since it is humanity's use and abuse of the planet that has brought it about. This is why environmentalists point out that their concerns are only likely to carry weight if nature is valued for its own sake. It requires another view of the natural world to the scientific - a moral one of intrinsic value.

The sense of wonder that leads to a feeling for nature's value is what is referred to as the sublime. Nature is called sublime, as opposed to beautiful or ugly, when it evokes awe: the limitless horizon, the towering wave, the looming cliff are common tropes evoked in art to convey this sublimity. Again, there is some philosophical debate as to the significance of the sublimity of nature. On one account, it reveals the limits of the human capacity to grasp it. On another, it reveals the amazing possibility that reason can get a grip on it at all. However, within both accounts, is the sense that the sublime expresses something of the value of nature that is intrinsic to it. The ancient philosopher Longinus expressed this connection well when he wrote:

> For grandeur produces ecstasy rather than persuasion in the hearer; and the combination of wonder and astonishment always proves superior to the merely persuasive and pleasant. This is because persuasion is on the whole something we can control, whereas amazement and wonder exert invincible power and force and get the better of every hearer.

The point is that the sublime does not try to convince; it simply overwhelms. It is as if nature always retains the capacity to express herself in quakes and infernos, in tiny intricacies and empty infinities, which vastly exceed the test tubes and equations that the scientific method must use to scrutinise her. She shows that she is fundamentally a law unto herself, and to be respected as such. This is one recognition that might lead to wonder.

Second, consider the way in which scientific knowledge must be connected to matters of which it itself has no grasp. In 2005, the TV naturalist, David Attenborough, broadcast his series, *Life in the Undergrowth*, in which he turned his camera on the world of invertebrates. It was both beautiful and fascinating to watch. However, it was not just the giant millipede that can kill a baby or the exquisite film of running ants that was gripping. There was a profound sense of wonder that pervaded the programmes. This led naturally - and without the sentimental anthropomorphisms that are so easy to read into more cuddly creatures - to the contemplation, first, of the insignificance of human beings in relationship to the insect world, and second to a more profound appreciation of the value of these creatures than a strictly scientific analysis allows.

This is particularly valuable since it comes from biology. Attenborough pointed out not just that invertebrates were the first creatures to colonise the land. Nor that they established the foundations of the land's ecosystems and were able to transcend the limitations of their small size by banding together in huge communities of millions. He said that if the invertebrates were to disappear today, the land's ecosystems would unavoidably, and rapidly, collapse. If human beings and all other back-boned animals similarly vanished, the world would continue without faltering.

He was also amazed at the behaviour caught on film.

I think the thing that surprises you is that when you watch invertebrates normally, say spiders, you think, 'well, they're just spiders and mechanical little creatures'. But when you start to film them, you discover that they have individual personalities. I mean, you can watch spiders of the same species, and some are lazy, some are hard working, some don't like light. They all have personalities, there's no doubt about it.

That is a wonderful but scientifically incomprehensible thing to say of insects!

Set Attenborough's thoughts alongside the seventeenth-century clergyman and poet, Thomas Traherne. He was also fascinated by the world opened up by new optical techniques - in his case not cameras but microscopes - and the way they revealed hidden wonders. The magnified sight of the 'curious and high stomached' fly caught his imagination in particular. Their 'burnished and resplendent' bodies like 'orient gold or polished steel' evoked a virtual encomium from his pen.

The infinite workmanship about his body, the marvellous consistence of his limbs, the most neat and exquisite distinction of his joints, the subtle and imperceptible ducture of his nerves, and endowments of his tongue, and ears, and eyes, and nostrils; the stupendous union of his soul and body, the exact and curious symmetry of all his parts, the feeling of his feet and the swiftness of his wings, the vivacity of his quick and active power ...

Traherne continues at some length. And the effect of his praise, not unlike the natural history film, is a growing admiration, even fondness, for

Illus. 3.2: The 'burnished and resplendent' fly, as drawn by Robert Hooke, in 1667.

the 'sucking parts' and 'buzzing wings' of these dipterous insects. That would be remarkable enough. But, like Attenborough contemplating the spider, Traherne's thoughts lead him further. So amazing is the fly, he writes, that it 'would make him seem like a treasure wherein all wonders were shut up together, and that God had done as much in little there, as he had done at large in the whole world.'

The point is that the 'personality of spiders' and the 'divine treasures' of the fly are not and never could be scientific descriptions. Write like that in a scientific journal, and you would be thought ridiculous. But these expressions of wonder do, nonetheless, convey real insight about the insects, the experience of studying them, and their significance in the world at large. One may ask why the fly has such 'infinite workmanship about his body'? The strictly scientific answer would incorporate details like the properties of chitin, the material from which insects' exoskeletons are made, and the evolutionary adaptation of its parts. But might one not also ask why the microscopic ridges of chitin on a butterfly wing, for example, refract light to produce colours that we spontaneously and admiringly call iridescent? Or why the chitin of the cicada produces a noise that we say can sing? Is it going too far to suggest that it is because they are not only wonderful to the human imagination but, in some unimaginable sense, aesthetically attractive to an insect mate? Just what that might mean is impossible to say. It is an example of a natural mystery within biology. A Darwinist 'explanation' that the wing and the song are sexually selected implicitly dismisses the wonder. But capturing a sense of it is surely part of the reason that Attenborough and Traherne's portraits of invertebrates are so compelling.

This, then, suggests a way in which wonder reconnects a strictly empirical form of scientific knowledge with other insights. Far from implying that scientific discourse has a natural authority over other sorts, it positively encourages the movement between the scientific, the metaphorical, the aesthetic, and even the theological. As Baron von Hügel, the theologian, wrote:

Only through such a consciousness of reality everywhere do we retain the feeling of mystery. For sheer conundrum is not mysterious, nor is a blank wall; but forests are mysterious, in which at first you observe but little, yet in which, with time, you see more and more, although never the whole; and the starry heavens are thus mysterious, and the spirit of man, and, above all, God, our origin and home.

In other words, to think that science challenges a sense of the sacred is to get it all wrong. When the limits of science are properly understood, the wonder science evokes positively encourages it.

The third feeling that wonder might inculcate is that of piety towards the cosmos. Piety commonly means the dutiful observance of religious rules and a devotion to the divine. Put less ecclesiastically, it is the sense that certain actions should be done, and certain attitudes should be respected, because they are a response to something that is given. The pious person is not a robot; they do not obey religious or quasi-religious rules unthinkingly. However, they are conscious that there is a wisdom in a tradition of piety, a wisdom that may prove particularly valuable in relation to the rashness that characterises overconfidence in human powers. Like Socrates, they respect the gods because it is an expression of the sentiment that, in spite of everything that can be explained about the world, much remains unknown.

A sense of piety comes into its own in the moral sphere. But even within the domain of science there are mysteries that might instill a similar sense. There are unknowns like time or gravity: scientific laws describe the form but not the cause, so these natural mysteries come to us as givens. There are unknowns like consciousness: science can posit certain conditions that are necessary but not sufficient for consciousness, so the experience of consciousness comes to us as a ground of our being. And there are unknowns like existence itself: why there is something rather than nothing is ultimately unanswerable by science, so existence can come to us as a gift.

Roger Scruton describes such piety as a humble debt of gratitude:

[P]iety means the deep down recognition of our frailty and dependence, the acknowledgement that the burden we inherit cannot be sustained unaided, the disposition to give thanks for our existence and reverence to the world on which we depend, and the sense of the unfathomable mystery which surrounds our coming to be and our passing away.

I think it would be fair to say that Einstein was pious in this way. Though not conventionally religious, neither was he atheistic. He did not fear being caught on the boundaries between science and religion where the sense of wonder seems most at home: 'Enough for me,' he wrote in *The World as I See It*, 'the inkling of the marvellous structure of reality, together with the single-hearted endeavour to comprehend a portion, be it never so tiny, of the reason that manifests itself in nature.' His piety is expressed in the suggestion that the greatest achievement of science is not to explain all but to point more clearly to that which is beyond explanation:

> The most beautiful and deepest experience a man can have is the sense of the mysterious. It is the underlying principle of religion as well as all serious endeavour in art and science. He who never had this experience seems to me, if not dead, then at least blind. To sense that behind anything that can be experienced there is a something that our mind cannot grasp and whose beauty and sublimity reaches us only indirectly and as a feeble reflection, this is religiousness. In this sense I am religious. To me it suffices to wonder at these secrets and to attempt humbly to grasp with my mind a mere image of the lofty structure of all that there is.

ETHICAL IMPORT

This then is the importance of wonder - its sense of intrinsic value, connection and piety - and I think it is implicitly agnostic. But can it be anything more than a private intuition? In terms of its ethical import, it might lead an individual to become a vegetarian, for example - out of a sense of not wanting to abuse sentient life. It might suggest to someone else that exponential carbon emissions are not just bad, because they destabilise the

planet, but that they are evil because they ruin it. However, to be of real use
at the present moment, wonder needs to be more than a personal sensibility, important though that is. To inform the debates of today - on the environment, on genetics, on technology - it must have wider public purchase.

Broadly speaking, debate about ethical issues in science is conducted
on two levels. One is the rational - the attempt to understand and then
think through issues in order to put down markers or principles from
which policy and law can be drawn. The other is intuitive - most commonly, the so-called 'yuk-factor' - the gut instinct which tells us that
something should not be done, lest a dangerous boundary is crossed
from which there would be no return.

The benefits of the first approach are, of course, massive. Decisions
can be informed, cognisant of change, and inclusive of the many stake-
holders whom the science affects. However, reason alone is not enough.
Beyond the obvious observation that people disagree, other factors limit
it. Modern science is often counterintuitive and hard to understand, so
that, for all the brilliance of popular science writers, significant swathes
of important subjects remain impenetrable to those outside the special-
ist circle. They are therefore hard to properly assess. Moreover, because
science is a reductionist discipline, it cannot but help open up gaps
between its own discourses and the human-centred ways that people
talk about the impact that science has on their lives. For example, when,
a couple of years back in the UK, there was widespread concern about
the risks associated with the MMR jab, scientists were relatively easily
able to rebut the research that had suggested there might be a connection
with autism. However, the question on parents' minds was by then
rather different; it was more like, how would I cope if my child did
become ill after the jab? Science could not address that.

Another reason that rational debate alone falls down is because of the
fact that being informed about things is not in itself enough to stop them
going wrong. Market forces, for example, might ride roughshod over sensible limits. Alternatively, there is the sense that knowledge itself can be
a dangerous thing: if it can be done, it will be done, is the thought here.

This is where intuitive sensibilities come in, and the yuk-factor in
particular. It is the public's gut concern about the techniques and appli-
cations of human cloning that currently prevents it from being legalised.

It was the emotional rejection of GM crops that prevented widespread planting in the UK, though not elsewhere in the world. The yuk-factor offers several advantages over reason alone. One is its power. For example, establishing tough governance of technological advance, in the form of laws or codes of conduct, is complicated for all sorts of reasons, not least because science operates in a global context and it is likely that the rules of one country can be sidestepped in another. The yuk-factor, though, may intimidate even the most gung-ho of scientists, severely reducing the appeal of 'going offshore'.

Another advantage of the yuk-factor is that it limits change that is driven by technological advance alone and forces wider moral factors to be considered. It asks the question, is society ready for this? Or, in a more positive vein, it may suggest that society has reached a point where such-and-such a technological possibility is desirable. The introduction of the contraceptive pill would be an example of this. In other words, the yuk-factor halts the inevitability implicit in the thought that because something can be done it should be done - partly by deploying gut instinct, partly by tapping into the conceptual frameworks that shape particular decisions. At best it represents a more holistic approach to ethics since it implicitly asks, who are we and what do we want life to be like.

However, the yuk-factor has its clear limitations too. One person's 'yuk' rejection is another person's 'yes' - a difference that becomes even more marked over the generations: test-tube babies once received the yuk treatment, for example. This implies not only that the yuk-factor provides shaky grounds for ethical norms but that it might at any given instant be wrong; it could be that popular opinion is merely catching up with scientific advance and that if the question was asked again a while later the opposite response would be given, though nothing substantial had changed.

Various combinations of the rational and intuitive are therefore often deployed in practice. The precautionary principle is a good case in point. This is the notion that if science cannot establish clearly that an action will have no adverse reaction, the action should not be taken. Such a cautious sensibility puts the burden of proof on doing something rather than doing nothing.

Cultivating Humility

It is in this mix that I believe the cultivation of wonderment might play a role. It would complement reason and intuition in ethical decision-making by highlighting wider questions of intrinsic value, connections and piety. It would both marvel and fear because of its consciousness of human limits. At best it would represent a mode of thought that embodies a kind of optimistic humility linked to a mode of feeling that embodies an inquisitive caution. Wonder stimulates the imagination and is also conscious of the dangers that come with a dogmatic attitude towards technological progress. It wants to know more and also knows that reductionist explanations are only part of the answer. It asks questions and also asks what kind of world is being created in the process. It puts 'why?' centre stage.

To put it in Socratic terms, wonder stems from the recognition that, although human beings are wiser than the animals, they are not as wise as gods. 'Playing God', if arguably inevitable in some cases, is only to be done with the upmost caution, for fear of hubris. When human beings are dabbling in things they don't fully understand, they are wise to resort to sources of moral wisdom. The wisdom inherent in wonder is its sense that some things have intrinsic value; that other sources of knowledge should have as much bearing as the scientific; and that an attitude of piety is appropriate in relation to things that whilst not inviolable are in some sense to be respected as given. As Piers Benn puts it in his examination of the idea of the sacred in Ben Rogers's fore-mentioned book: 'To reject *hubris* and to have a sense of piety - for want of a better expression - is to be conscious of our limitations in power and wisdom, and a sheer fragility of our lives and all that we care for.'

So how is this wonder manifest in practice? We have already considered sources of wonder within science itself: what the universe is made of; the irreducibility of phenomenon such as gravity and time; the spectacular image of flies; why there is something rather than nothing. In fact, although it sounds hifalutin when written about in abstract, it can be much more down to earth.

For myself, a sense of wonder became a part of my appreciation of science as a result of an undergraduate astronomy project. The aim of the exercise was to estimate the heights of mountains on the moon. This involved taking photographs of the lunar surface and measuring the lengths of the shadows that fell across its cliffs, peaks, valleys and plains. Calculating the height of the sun above the horizon, from the position of the mountain in question and the time of the photo, revealed something of our natural satellite's geography. My efforts were, of course, utterly trivial in the grand scheme of things. Today, lasers and radio waves are bounced off these grey peaks and can determine their elevation within meters. However, the exercise was worthwhile, even seminal, for me inasmuch as the thing I remember most was the experience itself. The photos had to be taken in the early hours of winter mornings, when the sky was clear, the moon was high and light pollution was low. Arising at 3 a.m. on dark, frosty mornings clothed the project with a sense of expectation: it reminded me of monks who say the office of Matins at similar hours as the people around sleep. Then there was the business of staring onto another world. The moon is a high-contrast place: with no obscuring atmosphere and pitted like pumice, it feels close through even a relatively low-powered telescope. Thomas Traherne imaged a 'celestial stranger' coming to earth and being amazed at its beauty. What he wrote of that can be said of such lunar observations too: 'Verily this star is a nest of angels! This little star so wide and so full of mysteries! So capacious and full of territories, containing innumerable repositories of delight when we draw near!' Not that we were simply gawping at it. The project cultivated a methodological precision in our observations, partly to gain as high-quality pictures as we could, and partly then to examine those images closely and select the best representative features for study.

An excellent sense of such wonderment also comes across in the best sci-fi films. Ridley Scott's *Blade Runner* is one movie that would fall into this category. The deep shadows and vivid colours of the cinematography, coupled to the ethereal music of Vangelis, mirrors the sense of awe of the replicants that Harrison Ford's character is chasing down. Thus, although they are regarded by the authorities as subhuman, Ford as the Blade Runner comes to respect them: his natural human superiority, which assumes that replicants are just to be killed, is humbled. The final scenes deliberately invoke an attitude of piety as Rutger Hauer, the leader of the replicants, presses a nail, Christ-like, into his hand in the effort fully to live out his last moments. What the movie and Philip K. Dick's novel that lies behind it achieve is not just the projection of a dystopian future but a critical reflection upon the way our science might go at present.

The movement between wonder, critique, ethics and humility also pervades the best popular science writing. In fact it is arguably the key ingredient in the genre's success. The physicist and author of books such as *The Mind of God*, Paul Davies, is also a winner of the Templeton Prize. In his address, he said: 'It is impossible to be a scientist working at the frontier without being awed by the elegance, ingenuity and harmony of the law-like order of nature. In my attempts to popularise science, I am driven by the desire to share my own sense of excitement and awe.' In an interview on the BBC programme *Devout Sceptics* he explained how this sense of wonder continues to drive him to keep asking the deepest 'why' questions.

> Why did we come to exist 13.7 billion years ago in a Big Bang? Why are the laws of electromagnetism and gravitation as they are? Why those laws? What are we doing here? And, in particular, how come we are able to understand the world? Why is it that we're equipped with intellects that can unpick all this wonderful cosmic order and make sense of it? It's truly astonishing.

Paul Davies is also one of those who does not allow hubris to run away with him. He resists the temptation to see in science a theory of everything. As he continued in his Templeton Prize address: 'We have to find a framework of ideas that ... yields a common set of principles around which peoples of all cultures can make ethical decisions yet remains honest in the face of scientific knowledge; indeed, that celebrates that knowledge alongside other human insights and inspirations.'

The thing that is particularly encouraging about these representations of wonder in popular culture is just that - they are popular. They do not depend upon a prior agreed common religious or ethical outlook, though they encourage an ethical even religious response. They pick up on a sense of humility in the face of our creatureliness. Scientific hubris has highly successful advocates too, of course: utopian sci-fi movies and evangelical Darwinian writers tend to replace human wonderment with human entitlement, scientific uncertainty with technological inevitability. But to wonder at the world seems to be as natural a thing to do in the technological age as it was in any other - perhaps even more so if we nurture it. The challenge is to educate this wonder so that it becomes a wisdom about living, that then shapes the choices that face us.

Wonderment as a framework within which to do moral philosophy is a long-term strategy. It encourages a way of thinking about ethics that depends first upon the development of a holistic view of life. In this way it contrasts with piecemeal reasoning on particular dilemmas - the more common way of making ethical decisions, and one that increasingly seems to be becoming impossible as more and more choices are forced upon people as a result of more and more technology being put at their disposal. In other words, it resonates with those approaches that seek to raise questions about the direction we are going in. It asks what is it to live, and not just what it is to live for longer? It asks what is it to be happy, and not just occupied or entertained? It asks how we can be fed, body *and* soul? It asks why we are so obsessed with security and what would truly address that? It is Socratic. Moreover, this approach is perhaps more significant than it might first seem when set against the ideological and economic powers that apparently set the scientific agenda, and are responsible for the pursuit of technology for its own sake. For if market forces decide where resources are spent, it is people who ultimately lie behind those market forces. Wonderment is something everyone can 'do', and to that extent it democraticises the appropriation of science. Perhaps it is already shaping the direction of future developments.

It is an approach that also has a fine pedigree. No less a scientific figure than Francis Bacon offered a kind of summary of its wisdom in three principles to be remembered when turning to science for answers.

> The first, that we not so place our felicity [happiness] in knowledge as we forget our mortality: the second, that we make application of knowledge to give ourselves repose and contentment and not distaste or repining: the third, that we do not presume by contemplations of nature to attain the mysteries of God.

Bacon advocates the benefits of a clear comprehension as to what science can and cannot achieve and understand, and a humbly minded wonderment. It is as necessary at this moment in the scientific age as it was when he wrote at the start.

BAD FAITH: RELIGION AS CERTAINTY

Ah, what a dusty answer gets the soul
When hot for certainties in this our life!

George Meredith

THAT SUNDAY IN SEPTEMBER ostensibly began for me like many
others since I had been a curate at St Cuthbert's Church, Billingham. I
arose early. Few people were about. To my back was the huge chemical
works that employed the parishioners and poisoned the air. In front of me
was a scene from the country. I could see the row of cottages, uneven with
age, including the one I lived in. At the end was the handsome vicarage
with its own drive. And then there was the Saxon church itself, so old that
some of its stones had been moved to the British Museum on account of
their Celtic inscriptions.

I walked in through the vestry door. The vicar had already arrived. I
walked down the north aisle to the bell rope in the tower. Its thick walls
were a little damp, the source of a moist smell that somehow linked the
present with the past. I rang the Angelus, the call to prayer that had
once stopped labourers in their fields, and was now, at least, keeping the
rumour of God alive.

After morning prayer, we prepared the vestments, the altar, the sacred
vessels and our stalls. St Cuthbert's was what is called Anglo-Catholic: it
was inspired by the famous sermon of Bishop Frank Weston of Zanzibar
who closed the Anglo-Catholic Congress of 1923 with the following stirring words: 'You have got your Mass, you have got your Altar, you have
begun to get your Tabernacle. Now go out into the highways and hedges
where not even the Bishops will try to hinder you. Go out and look for

Jesus in the ragged, in the naked, in the oppressed and sweated, in those who have lost hope, in those who are struggling to make good.'

That Sunday, I reflected upon the first time I celebrated the Mass myself, two and a half years earlier. Then was a time of optimism, when my hope was as strong as the incense that hung in the air; when my faith mirrored that of the people. I had entertained intellectual doubts about Christianity at theological college. However, once ordained, at least at first, worrying over the literal veracity of this or that doctrine seemed a distraction from the certainty of the mystery they tried to express: God is love. We could sing because our future, and the world's, was destined to be caught up in that divine and constant care.

But the next Sunday was entirely different. I did not ring the Angelus or lay out the vestments. I was 200 miles away, in Bath, staying with friends, having left the church. I felt free. I felt that, perhaps for the first time, I had made a decision that could be called grown-up. That previous Sunday had been my last. Six months before I had converted - to atheism. Now, my notice had been served, pastoral niceties had been performed, and my new Sunday ritual was bedding down fast: newspapers, coffee and conversation. Did I miss St Cuthbert's? Only in the way a teenager misses the presence of parents during their first days away from home. No more did I need to breathe an atmosphere thick with theism, I thought. I would rely on the heady drafts that were human and only human. For the next while a new certainty framed my life: life is all there is. The challenge is to live it.

So what had happened in between Billingham and Bath? How could it be that an individual with a sense of God clear enough to be ordained moves, within months, to the other side? What brings about such a change of heart?

The answer, of course, is complex and can be told in many ways. It was, in part, loneliness on the job. It was, in part, anger at the conservative attitudes of the Church. It was, in part, the shock of wearing a dog collar and having to be an ambassador for the institution. And it was also, in part, the triumph of scientific rationalism over theological deliberation. (This last factor was the one that seemed most important at the time since thinking of my leaving in this way made me feel in control.)

However, at another level, the leap was not so large or particularly complex. Before, my faith had depended upon the maintenance of a certain certainty. After, my newfound conviction re-established certainty, just in a different guise. Like a politician crossing the floor of the House, I may have switched parties but I was engaged in the same debate. 'How can you believe that?', the atheist berates the believer. 'How can you not believe that?', the theist despairs of the atheist. In terms of their convictions, theism and atheism are not worlds apart: epistemologically they may well share the same assumptions - that the world can be understood, that truth corresponds with reality, and that one can decide for or against God. 'Science offers the best answers to the meaning of life,' says Richard Dawkins. 'Is there more to life than this?', asks the evangelical Alpha Course - and you know they are not going to say no.

THE ATHEIST'S GOD

To be fair, there are some atheists who are not so sure. Julian Baggini is one. In his book, *Atheism: a Very Short Introduction*, he makes a rational case for not believing in God, or gods, not because he believes it is irrefutable nor because of some militant need to do so. Rather, atheism is the opinion he finds himself holding and, alongside the non-rational forces that inform his convictions, he believes he should have reasonable grounds for doing so. In fact, he opposes militant atheism because it undermines his more subtle position.

> I think that my opposition to militant atheism is based on a commitment to the very values that I think inspire atheism: an open-minded commitment to the truth and rational enquiry ... Hostile opposition to the beliefs of others combined with a dogged conviction of the certainty of one's own beliefs is, I think, antithetical to such values.

However, Baggini is exceptional in admitting such uncertainty. Most atheists who put their thoughts on paper are quite sure about the God they do not believe in. It is for this reason that the effect religion has on them is nothing short of emetic.

The journalist Martin Krasnik, who secured a rare interview with the novelist Philip Roth, made the mistake of asking him whether he was religious? 'I'm exactly the opposite of religious,' Roth erupted. 'I'm anti-religious. I find religious people hideous. I hate the religious lies. It's all a big lie.'

Polly Toynbee, a leading British newspaper columnist, routinely rounds on religion as a cause of evil. After the bombs in London, on 7 July 2005, she wrote: 'All religions are prone to it, given the right circumstances. How could those who preach the absolute revealed truth of every word of a primitive book not be prone to insanity? There have been sects of killer Christians and indeed the whole of Christendom has been at times bent on wiping out heathens.'

The polymath Jonathan Miller felt so strongly about it that he made a television series on the history of disbelief. He represents those for whom religion's supposed supernaturalism and belief in life after death is offensive. 'The notion is infantile. I'm amazed that people who can find their way to the toilet without advice can entertain such logically incoherent ideas,' he said in an interview with the London *Times*.

These champions of the Enlightenment are often far from rational in the way they bludgeon belief. Could someone who has sifted even a little of the evidence available still say with ease that religion is simply a lie, or that Christianity will spawn suicide bombers, or that religion is logically incoherent? Maybe the assertions are made only for the sake of their rhetoric force. But, if so, that only pushes the irrationality back a step for it raises the question why faith requires such overblown refutation. One is tempted to call into question the atheist's faith in reason.

There is also, I suspect, a deeper reason for their frustration and for God's irritating refusal to die. It is paradoxical. Like many religious people, many atheists want certainty in a sphere of existence in which certainty is not to be found. This means, in turn, that they focus their attacks on a series of man-made deities about which they can be certain because they have made them. Of course, these 'gods' - of lies, killers or infantile fools - are sometimes the same gods to which some religious people are prone. However, a moment's theological reflection shows that they are clearly false gods. The real challenge for the atheist, then, is to establish a knock-out blow for a decent conception of God. Even Julian Baggini, who resists the demonising way of attacking religion, still insists that religion is at fault for refusing to be judged by 'the standards of proof and evidence that intelligent discourse relies upon'. In other words, he would require a god he could believe in to be less than God, namely, subject to human reason. Little wonder that he remains an atheist.

The challenge for atheists has been articulated with great wit by Denys Turner, sometime Professor of Divinity in the University of Cambridge. His inaugural lecture to the Norris-Hulse chair was entitled 'How to be an atheist'. He has never met, he declared, an atheist who does not believe in a god that would be worth believing in to start with.

As an example of what he means consider the idea of God implicit in Nicholas Fearn's book, *Philosophy: the Latest Answers to the Oldest Questions*. It is a good book in many ways, seeking to take a general audience on a journey through what the greatest living philosophers have to say about being human. Fearn, who I presume to be an atheist, does not consider God a question to address head-on. Like belief in flying saucers or the power of crystals, I imagine he would say that to pay it serious attention would only be to pay it respect. However, given that God is one of the oldest questions humans have asked themselves, and that it is certainly a question plenty of philosophers are still asking, theological matters inevitably make several appearances in his book. This forces Fearn to get theological on occasion, which in turn exposes the divinity that he objects to as woefully reactionary and narrow-minded. His deity is an absolute principle that would underwrite human beliefs, guarantee meaning in life, and determine what everyone would do in the future. Conversely, it is divinity as inviolate moral will, punishing those who do wrong, and patting on the back those who do right. In other words, Fearn's theology says more about his atheism than it does about the question of God. It is a mirror opposite of the beliefs of a fundamentalist. Such people certainly exist. But they can hardly be taken as typical of the community of faith. And as to their theology - it might be sure but it is trite. Neither have anything but a reactionary conception of God.

GOD UNKNOWN

So what is it that atheists are missing? What would it be to have a reasonable conception of the divine? What idea of God might they have that any decent theology would not deny too?

Thomas Aquinas, the giant of medieval philosophy, provides the key. For any usual subject of human investigation, he says, there are two steps to take. First is to identify what the matter in hand is about, and second to define its nature and scope. For example, biology is about living things and its domain is the material world of the animal and plant kingdoms. Or, physics is about the natural world and its domain is the fundamental constituents of the universe. However, theology is different. It can say what it is about - God. But God is not like other things in nature and scope. If God could be investigated like living things or the natural world then God would not be God. Thomas wrote, 'since we cannot know of God what he is, but [only] what he is not, we cannot inquire into the how of God, but only into how he is not'. Thomas is, in this sense, radically and insistently agnostic about God. 'It is extremely difficult for readers of Aquinas to take his agnosticism about the nature of God seriously,' wrote Herbert McCabe:

> If he says 'Whatever God may be, he cannot be changing' readers leap to the conclusion that he means that what God is is static. If he says that, whatever God may be, he could not suffer together with (*sympathise* with) his creatures, he is taken to mean that God must be by nature unsympathetic, apathetic, indifferent, even callous. It is almost as though if Aquinas had said that God could not be a supporter of Glasgow Celtic, we supposed that he was claiming God as a Rangers' fan.

All that, though, would be wrong. Thomas Aquinas is merely but profoundly insisting what God is not. A thought experiment that he provides develops the idea further. Consider someone who decides to count up all the things that exist in the world. Calculator in hand, they start on everything they can see around them - trees, insects, people, buildings, books and so on. Eventually they reach a number, let us call it N. But just as they are sitting down, they realise they have missed something out. It happens that they believe in God. So they conclude, there must actually be N + 1 things in the world.

This is wrong, says Thomas. The answer is, in fact, N because God is not a thing at all. If that was the case, then the divine being could not also be the creator of all other things - something that is a minimal requirement for God to be considered a worthwhile deity. As Turner sums the thought experiment up: 'although the word "God" is not the proper name of an individual, but a word we *use* in the way in which we use descriptions, still we have no proper *concept* which answers to it. Having no proper concept of God, we have no way of identifying God as an *instance* of any kind.'

'PROOFS' OF GOD

This is also the meaning of Thomas's five so-called proofs for the existence of God. They can be put into two groups: the first four are called cosmological; the fifth is teleological. The cosmological arguments arise from looking at the cosmos and asking what lies behind it. Thomas saw that the cosmos exists, that it is full of movement, and that it is full of causes of movement. So he argued that there must be a necessary being, an unmoving mover and an uncaused cause behind it all, as it were, and that this being must have the attributes of a deity, whatever else that God might be. In a modern idiom, Thomas's questions are a bit like asking what caused the Big Bang, and concluding that it must have been something divine-like because the cause must have been before the Big Bang - when there was only divine-like being.

The teleological argument also arises from looking at the cosmos but, rather than looking at its origins, it looks at its purpose. It argues that the universe appears to be designed with an end in mind - whether that end be taken as the 'pinnacle of creation', namely man, or simply the intricacy of the universe itself (the version put most famously by William Paley in the analogy of finding a fine watch and concluding that there must, therefore, be a watchmaker).

As positive proofs, the cosmological arguments are highly vulnerable to critique. For example, one might ask what this God looks like, for clearly the unmoved mover and uncaused cause does not look at all like the personal God people claim to believe in. Someone else might think that if God can exist without a cause, then perhaps the universe can come into being without a cause too. (This is, in fact, what certain quantum cosmologists suggest - the universe simply sprang into being as a result of the Uncertainty Principle. The difficulty is that no-one really knows what the Uncertainty Principle means, so to say this of the universe only pushes the questions of existence one step back.)

The teleological argument can be made to look flimsy too. Most obviously, Darwinian theory suggests a mechanism by which plants and animals can come to look designed, but are not, since the 'design' is actually adaptive. By extension, the Darwinian supposes that the universe itself evolved according to natural, indifferent processes.

Thomas's point, though, is that to try to refute the so-called arguments for the existence of God is itself to mistake their purpose. His five ways are certainly supposed to show that it is reasonable enough to look at the cosmos and intuit a God behind and before it. But at the same time - and this is the crucial point the atheists miss - the five ways are simultaneously supposed to prove the impossibility of knowing anything positive about God. What Thomas intends is to instruct believers in why it is simply not possible to say much about what it means to confess that God exists.

For example, say that the universe did spring from nothing in a random fluctuation of the quantum vacuum. For the believer - following a modern version of Thomas's 'proof' - the implication is not that quantum theory disproves God, but that God's 'uncausedness' must be more mysterious still. Or consider the teleological argument from design. As Hume pointed out, thinking that a watch is made by a watchmaker presupposes that we already know who or what makes watches - namely, the fore-mentioned watchmaker. So whilst design in the universe might apparently be seen all over the place - from the fine-tuned organs of the senses to the fine-tuned constants of cosmology - the argument should also highlight the fact that any designer of the universe would be way beyond anything of which we might have experience. As Turner summaries again: whatever might show God to exist equally shows God's unknowability.

Missing this fundamental point is to make the same mistake as taking Socrates' question in the *Euthyphro* as an argument for atheism. This asked whether things are good because the gods say so, or whether they are good because they are good in themselves. If the former, then the suggestion is that this makes morality arbitrary. If the latter, as seems right, then it supposedly negates the gods' role in morality - which would seem to be a major blow. What is routinely missed is Socrates' point that the conundrum is not an issue for the gods, but for human beings. The importance of the question is to show up the limitations of human conceptions of morality. It says nothing about the gods' involvement with it.

THE LOSS OF CONTEMPLATION

No doubt the unknowability of God is very annoying to conviction atheists. Rather than see the conundrums it poses as an invitation to grapple with the limits of human knowledge, they reject them as incoherent. Another so-called argument for the existence of God, the ontological argument, makes the point directly. Formulated by St Anselm, it was meant by him as a kind of meditation on God. It is found in his work, the *Proslogion*. It is a kind of meditation that has the aim of trying to invoke as profound a sense as is possible of the enormous mystery of God in the human mind. The formula that Anselm derives to do this is that God is 'something than which nothing greater can be thought'. In other words, he suggests in his meditation: contemplate anything at all, and God is greater.

Anselm's ontological argument is often today summarised thus: if God must be greater than existence, God cannot, therefore, be thought not to exist. QED - God exists! Little wonder it comes across as nothing more than a trick of logic, which most philosophers agree as a proof it probably is. The atheists then set on it. They point out that it is only about the *concept* of God and God's existence, and this says nothing about what exists in the real world. Under the same logic, someone could develop a concept about the perfect example of anything - say a perfect car or a perfect flower - and then ask, why its perfection should not entail its existence too. Clearly, it would be a fool who then set out to find this perfect car in the showroom or perfect flower in the meadow. Therefore, they say, it is the fool who thinks the ontological argument proves God exists too.

The problem for the medieval 'proofs' of God is that, in the present day, it is easy to lose sight of the religious milieu in which their authors

Illus. 4.1: Fra Angelico's portrait of St Dominic comes from a time in which the practice of prayer and the exercise of reason were indistinguishable.

expected them to be pondered. The cloister has been replaced by the classroom; flickering candles by florescent lights; the prie-dieu by the projector. With these changes, the meditation comes to be taken as an argument - for the existence of God. If you are a believer, as Anselm was, then this is the start of a reflection on the nature of God's existence - since existence is the greatest attribute God can have. Certainly this is a reflection that would take the believer beyond reason, which is to say that it will throw up all kinds of rational conundrums. But then that is the whole point: if someone's thoughts on God seem logical, reasonable and clear, then only one thing can be said for sure; the meditation is not on God but on some concept of a reduced divinity.

AFTER ATHEISM

I can remember being similarly irritated by the insistence of theologians that to read the proofs about God in a literal way was to misread them. Logic is logic, I thought; bad logic is bad logic. By implication I also believed that reason was supreme, and human reason had replaced God. For a while, I concluded that if God's unknowability meant that anything that might be said about God is also a reason for not saying it at all, then that itself was good reason to be an atheist.

However, in time, atheism ceased to be, for me, such a desirable thing to assert though not because of any proofs. After all, proofs tend to confirm minds not change them. Rather, the complex of irrational and psychological ire that had fired my revulsion of God abated, and then died - for equally elusive and poorly understood reasons. Having said that, at least one thought did stand out in my mind during this time that is worth remarking on. Part of the reason that atheism lost its appeal was because I became increasingly conscious that to be an atheist seemed to entail denying more than I really wanted to or, in truth, felt. This question kept occurring to me: like the atheist who refuses to see Anselm's argument as a meditation, and so misses the point of it, was my atheism refusing all sorts of imaginative possibilities in life?

I recall being on holiday in Egypt and being truly amazed not just at the remains of the temple at Karnak, but also at how they inspired a sense of religious awe in me - and no doubt thousands of other tourists - for all that we live 4000 years later in time. In the guide book, I read about the social and economic significance of temple architecture and the religious system. But this description, though interesting from the perspective of the human sciences, seemed to miss the most signifi- cant element of all - the awesome spirit of the place. Did I want to limit my appreciation of these other, ancient people to essentially atheistic discourses? It is not that an agnostic or theist could have an experience of ruins that is not open to the atheist. But there did seem to me to be something in atheism that would prefer to turn its back on such an experience perhaps because to embrace it would be to be embarrassed by the confession of being so moved by the worship of ancient deities.

I had a similar sense in relation to religious music. Such music has an ability to speak, without words, directly to the soul, suggesting at the same time that, through the senses, the soul is being opened to that which lies way beyond it. Clearly such an understanding of music can be debated. But allowing it for now, it does express how I felt that reli- gious music seemed different from other forms of art, and even secular music. A Mozart aria of passionate intensity might make you weep in the way it captures the longings of your heart; a Hopper painting of solipsistic isolation might do as much by reminding you of your own loneliness; a movie might make you cry through empathic sentimental- ity. But religious music need not say anything that can be connected to your past or present, but still it can move you to tears in apparently nameless ways.

Again, an interpretation determined by the human sciences seems just too parochial. It would ask the question what religious music is *for*, as if its effect can be summed up by saying it binds people together, like a nationalistic hymn. Or it might adopt a psychological explanation, saying it evokes some altered state of consciousness, as if the altered state were all. However, such understandings alone, whilst illuminating to a degree, seem to necessitate certain 'no-go' areas of thought - those that resort to theology. Again, this is not to say that only believers can fully appreciate the perfection of Bach's B minor mass or Mozart's Requiem, for clearly believers do not gain some extra musical faculty upon turning to God. There is no divine hearing aid. Rather, it is the atheist mindset that is at fault: it appears forced to put a cap on the appreciation of such things. At the very least, a degree of agnosticism in relation to the value of religious yearning would seem to be necessary to be open to the music that speaks of divinity.

I came to believe that the certainty of my atheism thwarted my imagination; in practice, for fear of compromising its integrity, it led to a poverty of spirit. When the certainty of my atheism slipped, all sorts of thoughts became possible once again.

THE GIFT OF CREATION

Turner's advice to atheists on how best not to believe in God adds to this sense of the poverty that conviction atheism seems to entail. Turner has shown that, contrary to what many atheists might think, their denial of certain kinds of divinity is, in fact, exactly the same denial any reasonable theist would make too. The difference comes because the atheist stops there, whereas the theist will go on to see whether anything affirmative can be said about this unknowable God. In other words, if theists would deny most of the things about a deity that atheists deny too, then when does the point come at which theists affirm something that atheists would still deny? The positive thing that theists would assert, and that atheists presumably would not, Turner believes, is that the world is created. The world is *not* 'just there', as the atheistically inclined Bertrand Russell put it.

Of course, the belief that the world is created does not mean that the theist can say anything much about *how* the world is created; that is part of the unknowability of the creator. Neither does it make any difference to the way that, say, the sensible theist will want to do science; this is not an argument for Intelligent Design. However, there is more entailed by the atheist's denial than merely the assertion that the world is brute fact.

The difference comes because if the atheist denies that the world is created, they also resist the idea of existence as gift. Turner explains it this way:

> In saying that the world is created out of nothing, you are beginning to say that the world comes to us, our existence comes to us, from an unknowable 'other'; that is to say, you are claiming that existence comes to us as pure gift, that for the world to exist just *is for it to be created.*

One might think about the difference this makes in a thought experiment. Imagine a customer who logs onto their bank account one morning and sees an unexpected balance of $1 million. Being an upright individual, they alert the bank. However, after an investigation, the balance stays the same: no mistake has been made, they are told. The customer can reach one of three conclusion. The first is to conclude that the money is a gift from some unknown benefactor. The second is to conclude that the new balance is the result of a glitch but that, luckily, the money is now theirs. The third is to be unsure about what has happened: it could be luck or it could be a gift.

The first conclusion is like the theist's response to existence: they are full of gratitude for the gift. The second conclusion is like the atheist's response: having no-one to thank, they merely count themselves very lucky. The third conclusion is like the agnostic's response: they would perhaps spend some of the money trying to find a benefactor to give thanks to, though they never completely puzzle it out.

The difference between a response of gratitude and a response of luck to existence also carries implications for how an individual thinks about the world around them. For the response of luck tends to foreclose the exploration of existence, particularly when that involves entertaining thoughts that bring up theological problems. They will tend to think that there is little point in asking questions for which answers 'in principle' cannot be given. So, and recalling the money analogy again, the question of life becomes only how to spend or use it. The response of gratitude, in contrast, is in practice more expansive since it longs to know more about this gift of existence and what lies behind, above and through it - for all that such questions can never be wholly satisfied.

BACK TO CHURCH?

Now, it would be fair, after my rejection of the certainties of atheism, to ask why I did not return to some kind of Christianity. I'd moved from the certain world of the young priest, to the certain world of the turncoat atheist, and had now seen through both. Mightn't the discovery that any decent talk about God should include a sense of God's unknowability - indeed must make that its main objective for fear of worshipping lesser gods and idols - signal a return to a more mature theistic commitment?

The answer, in brief, is that moving on from atheism gave me permission, as it were, to re-engage a religious imagination - Schleiermacher's sense and taste for the Infinite, Tillich's quest for the ground of being. However, it did not easily re-engage a belief in the Christian God. The position I had come to was an appreciation of the unknowability of the divine. This left me passionately agnostic. As it happened, I did try going to church - thinking that if I picked the right one it might be a good place to allow my new-found uncertainties to flourish into a way of life. However, what I had not reckoned with was the repeated expressions of doctrinal certainties that pepper the vast majority of contemporary church services. They are not the same as the assertions of the fundamentalist. But to an agnostic, they are no less hurdles to surmount.

The very first words you are likely to hear upon attending a mass, communion, worship or family service are either, 'In the name of the Father, the Son and the Holy Spirit', or, 'The Lord be with you' - phrases that immediately encompass all sorts of assertions about God. Then there will be the prayers of intercession, the part of the service where the concerns of the world and the people are rehearsed. I have no problem with this as a practice; it is a natural thing to want to do. My problem is the terms in which these prayers are often couched: the assumption is that the Christian has a personal relationship with God, not dissimilar to the relationship one might have with a best friend, an assumption that strikes me as a quagmire of delusion. Personally, I also find the words of many hymns problematic - when they read more like pop lyrics than poetry. And then there is the main stumbling-block in the service when people are invited to recite the creed - 'I believe in God ...' and so on. Even uttering the *credo* - the 'I believe' - leaves me wanting to add qualifiers. By the end - 'the holy catholic church, the communion of saints, the forgiveness of sins, the resurrection of the body, and the life everlasting' - I have run out of fingers to cross.

There are a number of rejoinders that the minister or priest would suggest in response to these complaints. First, it might be said that a church is a Christian place of worship - for believers - and so one should only expect Christian language to be used there. That is fair comment. But my difficulty is not so much with the Christian nature of the language. After all, there is no such thing as generic religious language: it always originates in specific traditions that inevitably have a certain hue. This is why agnosticism and atheism are recognisably related to the religious systems that they are struggling with or objecting to. My difficulty is more with the tone of the language; its seemingly unguarded affirmations.

There are services that are exceptions to this. For example, at the midnight mass of Christmas, the story of the birth and the time of day both work to put a narrative in the foreground, not statements of belief. Alternatively, cathedral worship, with its glorious music and architecture, gains the advantage that the aesthetic content of the liturgy eclipses its doctrinal content. Might it be that the persistent popularity of these kinds of service, amidst otherwise declining congregations, has something to do with the way they allow the spiritual search of the agnostic? (In similar mood, I sometimes wonder whether a return of the Latin mass might do wonders for numbers. It would be an advantage to hear the beauty of the language without comprehending the words.)

A different rejoinder would emphasise the point that religious language is always part of a tradition. Take the creed. It is a historic formulary that originated at a particular moment in the Church's history. Today it should be read as an expression of the Church's connection with the past and its continuity over time. That is true. But as a historic formulary, it was specifically designed to define who was orthodox and unorthodox. It not only achieved its purpose then but achieves the same effect today - forcing the agnostic out of their closet. (I have also heard it said that the creed should be read as a hymn of praise, but it is surely too bureaucratic for that: it was written by committee and sounds like it too.)

A final rejoinder would want to correct the perception of religious language as straightforwardly affirmative. The fundamental point here would be that all religious language is metaphorical, in keeping with the insight that God is radically unknowable. Now, there are various strategies that religious language can use to underline its metaphorical nature. Sometimes negative language is used. For example, God might be said to be 'immortal' or 'invisible' - that is not mortal and not visible, with the emphasis on the *not*. Alternatively, when positive statements about God are used, they should never occur in isolation, but should be set alongside other statements that unsettle any direct inferences. For example, when God is called 'Lord', it is quite clear that he is not a lord in any usual sense - dressed in ermine or lording it over an estate - but that the word is metaphorically trying to express something of God's authority or power. Similarly, when God is called Father, Son and Holy Spirit, the idea is to convey insights in the way that God is manifest to human beings, at least as the Christian tradition sees its. The emphasis, again, is on the way God is manifest *to human beings* - that is, though divinely inspired, this is human language about God. What God is in Godself is as mysterious as ever. As the Archbishop of Canterbury, Rowan Williams, put it in a lecture entitled 'What Is Christianity?', at the international Islamic University in Islamabad: 'When we speak of "the Father, the Son and the Holy Spirit", we do not at all mean to say that there are three gods - as if there were three divine people in heaven, like three human people in a room.'

The Archbishop's thought must be right. However, it is one thing to say that technically speaking the doctrine of the Trinity does not include the idea that there are three gods. But it is another thing entirely for the language to force the individual beyond the idea that God is literally Father or Lord. I can only speak from experience, but I doubt whether many Christians think that, or would even think it right to think that. Most think of God as a Father, as Lord.

So my problem is that the modern use of religious language has sidelined the unknowability of God - in favour of more accessible notions of the divine. Further, this, I suspect, is part of a general historical shift in which a full sense of theological agnosticism has largely been forgotten - not only in the sense of having been marginalised but even in the sense of having been lost. To see this, we must take a step back and look at the history of ideas that lies behind modern Christianity, the path that has led to contemporary Church language and practice.

MYTH AND LOGOS

It was a few hundred years ago that it first started to look as if a gap might be opening up between a scientific understanding of the world and the Christian one, after Copernicus displaced the earth from the centre of the universe. What we now call the scientific revolution had begun. It would be a mistake to think that from that moment on it was only a question of time until atheism ruled the day, as if the earth's demotion obviously entailed God's destruction too. Many scientists continued and continue to see God in their observations and experiments. Like Newton, they thought that the new science revealed God to them more clearly.

However, something profound has shifted in this time. A scientific way of talking about things has gained the upper hand. This began with the tremendous success of scientific descriptions of the natural world - a success that some, namely adherents of scientism, would like to see extended to every sphere of life, usurping God once and for all. However, whilst science can now, I believe, be seen to have lost this war over explanation - because it overreaches itself when it claims that everything is explicable by a rationalist materialism - the arrival of modern science has changed the terms of the debate.

The move is described very well by the historian of religions, Karen Armstrong. In a nutshell she sums it up by saying that the scientific revolution led to the triumph of *logos* over myth. *Logos* - Greek for word, argument, speech and reason - is the worldview that latches onto facts and, in particular, those facts that have practical application. It is the natural language of the sciences. Myth - from the Greek *muthos*, meaning a story that is symbolic, traditional or paradoxical - is the worldview that grapples imaginatively and intuitively with the significance of patterns, places and values in successive variants of mythological stories. It is the natural language of religion. Myth does not sit easily alongside a strident *logos* if it repeatedly asks myth to declare whether its stories are realistic and logical, true or false. This is the way in which science has changed the terms of the debate. It forces a focus on pragmatic outcomes - results, measurements and reason. It squeezes out and displaces thoughts that are indissoluble, irreducible and uncertain.

The distinction offers another reason why science, the mode of thought that quintessentially exemplifies *logos*, fails as meaning. In *A Short History of Myth*, Armstrong writes:

> Thanks to their scientific discoveries, [people] could manipulate nature and improve their lot. The discoveries of modern medicine,

hygiene, labour-saving technologies and improved methods of transport revolutionised the lives of Western people for the better. But *logos* had never been able to provide human beings with the sense of significance that they seemed to require. It had been myth that had given structure and meaning to life, but as modernisation progressed and *logos* achieved such spectacular results, mythology was increasingly discredited. As early as the sixteenth century, we see more evidence of a numbing despair, a creeping mental paralysis, and a sense of impotence and rage as the old mythical way of thought crumbled and nothing new appeared to take its place. We are seeing a similar anomie today in developing countries that are still in the earlier stages of modernisation.

So the relationship between *logos* and myth is not a matter of choice - as if for certain parts of life one can resort to the scientific, and for other parts one can turn back to myth. Because scientific *logos* compromises the potency of myth, modern people in search of meaning appear to be presented with a zero-sum game with a lust for certainty winning out.

Myth, though, is not the sum total of Christianity: it is many things - an aesthetic, a set of metaphysical beliefs, a response to the vicissitudes of life, a communal or ethnic identity, as well as a set of mythological stories. This means that there is good news and bad news for the believer. The good news is that, when *logos* gains the upper hand, it does not bring Christianity to an end: removing the power of myth is not the knock-out blow that the atheist might hope because Christianity has plenty of other *raisons d'être*, not least its unique abilities as a response to life and as a provider of identity. It is for this reason that it continues to be a major force in human life. Only the most militant atheists can think otherwise at the start of the twenty-first century. Even in relatively secular countries like the UK, where few people go to church, many, perhaps a majority, still want the church to be part of the fabric of their lives.

THE THEIST'S GOD

However, if science has not forced out belief, it has forced Christianity to change: in the *logos*-centric world, it is compelled to speak the language of fact and application. This, I suspect, is the underlying reason that religious services are now dominated by doctrinal statements about God. Doctrine is religion 'as fact'; it is religion 'applied'. Transformed in this way, it tries to fulfill the two main criteria required by science: the need to deliver certainty and the need to deliver relevance.

Think of the ramifications of this for the doctrine of the Trinity. It originated in the era of myth, the fourth century, when, as Karen Armstrong continues, it was quite natural for Gregory, Bishop of Nyssa, to explain that

> Father, Son and Spirit were not objective, ontological facts, but simply 'terms that we use' to express the way in which the 'unnameable and unspeakable' divine nature adapts itself to the limitations of our human minds. You could not prove the existence of the Trinity by rational means. It was no more demonstrable than the elusive meaning of music or poetry.

However, since the sixteenth century, this cannot but help sound like a cop-out; it sounds like the theologian is avoiding the responsibility of saying whether or not the Trinity is true: *logos* demands a decision. Thus, when Christians confess belief in a Triune God now, they do not take it as a reminder that God should *not* be thought of in personal terms, because the personal dimension to the human-divine relationship comes from human beings, not God. Quite the opposite: God, it is said, must be personal to be relevant to me. So the Trinity is taken as describing God in Godself: in practice, and reflected in the writings of some theologians, God is literally a Father, literally Son, literally Holy Spirit. To do anything else would mean that the doctrine fails according to the rules of *logos*, which in the modern age is to say it fails, period. (This is also why apologists, like the Archbishop of Canterbury, are forced to tell other monotheists that, in spite of appearances, Christians are not polytheists.)

The pressure to drop myth and take up *logos* explains many other features of modern Christianity too. It explains the extraordinary success of evangelicalism. This is nothing if not religion as fact and with direct personal applicability. In evangelicalism, the individual must decide what they think about Jesus - who he was - not as part of some lifelong engagement with a

tradition, as Christian writers of the past thought of it, but as a one-off
assessment of the evidence. As the TV evangelist demands, look at the
witness of the Bible: the rational person can only come to one of three
conclusions - either Jesus was mad, bad or who he said he was! The thought
that the Gospels of the New Testament might have been written not to
provide factual evidence but as the struggles of four uncertain individuals,
or groups of individuals, continually working out who Jesus was, does not
occur to this school of thought (or, if it does, it is branded liberal nonsense).
Indeed, that there are four Gospels that in part do not agree should be a
source of inspiration for Christians, not a cause of obfuscatory embarrass-
ment. The disagreements remind the reader that the Bible points beyond.

Having delivered on the factual requirement for modern belief, evangelicalism also delivers on the requirement of relevancy. 'Do you accept
Jesus Christ as your personal Lord and Saviour?', 'Are you born again?',
'What would Jesus do?' - these are the questions of a personal religion
that must be seen to be applicable to the modern, autonomous individual. Similarly, courses on being a Christian at work, being a Christian at
home, marriage as a Christian, singleness as a Christian - these are the
self-help programmes that a church must run to be relevant. Or again:
evangelicals routinely believe they can talk to God as easily as they can
call their mother. This is an idea of prayer that is more or less absent in
the spiritual traditions of the past. Then prayer was perceived as enter-
ing a cloud of unknowning or a dark night of the soul. Now, though,
prayer is the activity described in Wendy Cope's poem, from her collection *Serious Concerns*:

When I went out shopping,
I said a little prayer:
'Jesus, help me park the car
For you are everywhere.'

Even within so-called liberal churches, the *logos* is profoundly shaping the
nature of the church. Paul Fletcher's book, *Disciplining the Divine*, explains
why from a historical perspective. He points out that one of the key
tenets of the Reformation was that the Bible should take precedent in
matters of doctrine and salvation, over the tradition and the Church. *Sola*

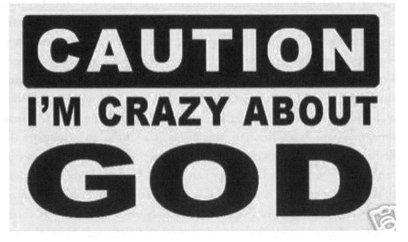

Illus. 4.2: Apophatic religion was a life-long search. Fundamentalist religion is a stick-on statement.

scriptura was the slogan. Unless something can be proven in the Bible, it cannot be taken as 'gospel truth'. The element that the Bible could provide, and that the diverse tradition and a corrupt Church could not, was the new, post-Copernican need for fact, decision and certainty.

However, treating the Bible in this way is a risky strategy because the Bible itself could be put under the microscope and subjected to the rigours of scientific investigation - as, indeed, it was - and as, indeed, it was found to be wanting. What then? How might the integrity of the Bible as a source of authority be preserved? It came to be thought of as embodying a different sort of reason by the Reformers - a divine reason that contains certainties of which secular science knows nothing. No longer was Jesus the Word (as, paradoxically, the Bible itself testifies); the Bible was. 'This is the Word of the Lord,' Christians now say after the Bible is read out in services - in mainstream practice, not just fundamentalist churches. In other words, the scientific revolution forced Christians to turn to the Bible, and it forced them to say that the Bible was above the critique of the scientific worldview.

This, in turn, sheds light on crises the churches face today. Consider the issue that appears to be tearing the Anglican Church apart - that of homosexuality. It is often a puzzle to people why gay relationships should be so divisive. Jesus himself said nothing about same-sex activity. It should not be a 'first-order' issue, like say the Trinity or the Incarnation. Surely, it would be thought, an essentially liberal Church ought to be able to find an accommodation within which homosexuality is treated as a matter of private conscience. However, homosexuality has become a schismatic issue today because it has become a test case of this need for biblical certainty. Liberal voices contest this, arguing that the Bible condemns the consumption of shellfish and the practice of usury, or that the word homosexuality is a modern one and has little to do with the same-sex activity objected to in the New Testament. But, to the conservative, they miss the point. Homosexuality, they say, is against the order of creation described in the Bible, expressed no more succinctly than in the book of Genesis. The argument that the Pope, Archbishops, Chief Pastors and Moderators make in mainstream churches is that God created humans as man and woman in a complementary relationship, and that this ordering of human relationships represents a line beyond which a Christian cannot go. To condone homosexual relationships, as if they were a similarly ordained part of creation, is therefore read as a rejection of the Bible *in toto*. This is what the culture of certainty puts the liberal Christian up against.

A similar rationale also explains why creationism carries such force in the US. A literal seven days of creation is taken as a key test of faith; if you believe in it, you believe in the Bible; if not, you do not.

Sexuality is not the only issue over which churches are forced to draw the line. One of Pope Benedict XVI's favourites is relativism. The growth of relativism is another paradoxical product of the scientific revolution. In the search for facts and certitude, philosophical certainty is itself called into question, and flounders. Only one thing is sure, relativism says: nothing is sure (that this is itself a contradiction does nothing to lesson the fear of the nihilism relativism implies). The Pope objects to this. But what is particularly surprising, for a man who confesses faith in God, is the ferocity with which he rails against it. 'We are moving towards a dictatorship of relativism which does not recognise anything as definitive and has as its highest value one's own ego and one's own desires,' he said in a sermon on the eve of his election. 'From Marxism to free-market liberalism to even libertarianism, from collectivism to radical individualism, from atheism to a vague religion, from agnosticism to syncretism and so forth.' The reason this is surprising from the Pope is that talk of God - theology - is itself bound to embody a kind of relativism because anything that can be said about God is provisional - relative to human beings' incapacity to know God. However, in a world of science, lines must be drawn in the sand. Rampant relativism is a good candidate for demonisation. Everyone fears it a little. It seems to be thought that if the price is the rejection of religious uncertainty, and forgetfulness about the ultimate unknowability of God, then that is a price worth paying. So strange as it may seem, papal infallibility is as much a product of the scientific revolution as Darwinism. It is surely no coincidence that the doctrine was formulated in 1870, just 11 years after the publication of *On The Origin of Species*.

OTHER FUNDAMENTALISMS

My discussion has focussed on Christianity, reflecting my own experience. Christianity is, arguably, particularly prone to the influence of science because, although it has a fantastically rich, if increasingly forgotten, mythological heritage, it has always been the case that what makes someone a Christian is assenting to creedal statements. In this way, it is unlike the other religions of the book - Islam and Judaism - within which what one does, as well as what one believes, counts. For them, orthopraxis - the correct performance of rituals - has always counted alongside orthodoxy in determining faithfulness.

However, the culture of certainty is radically shaping contemporary Judaism and Islam too. In Islam, it is Wahhabism that is the parallel to fundamentalism and that sets the tone. As the Muslim scholar Reza Aslan says in his book, *No God but God: the Origins, Evolution and Future of Islam*, Wahhabism should have been 'a spiritually and intellectually insignificant movement in a religion principally founded upon spiritualism and intellectualism'; 'it is not even considered true orthodoxy by the majority of Sunni Muslims'. Yet its ideological certainty has an appeal that is seriously compromising what Aslan takes to be Islam's historic pluralism.

> Islam is and has always been a religion of diversity. The notion that there was once an original, unadulterated Islam that was shattered into heretical sects and schisms is a historical fiction. Both Shi'ism and Sufism in all their wonderful manifestations represent trends of thought that have existed from the very beginning of Islam, and both find their inspiration in the words and deeds of the Prophet. God may be One, but Islam most definitely is not.

Indeed, the central doctrine of *tawhid* in Islamic theology - the profession that 'There is no god but God' - is itself in part a formula for preventing ideas of God becoming fixed. Notice how the first phrase, 'There is no god', sits uneasily alongside the second, 'but God'. On the one hand, it is a statement of the truths the Muslim believes were revealed by the Prophet. But, on the other hand, it is also a statement that God is greater still - *Allahu Akbar!* (literally, God is greater). 'Tawhid suggests that God is beyond any description, beyond any human knowledge', explains Aslan. He laments the fact that bigotry and fanaticism are the new false idols in Islam.

The same can be said of Judaism. Although there is no equivalent movement that stands out to the extent of Wahhabism or Christian
fundamentalism, there is an issue around which religious conservatives can
rally and exert influence, that of the politics of the state of Israel.
Thankfully, there is a lighter side to this too. I was once told the joke, by a
rabbi, about an orthodox Jew and a gentile caught in a lift on the Sabbath.
Being in Jerusalem, the lift had two sets of controls. One control had normal switches to operate the lift. The other had a set of a buzzers, that did
not start the lift, but prompted a non-orthodox operator to do so. Why the
buzzers? They meant that, on the Sabbath, the orthodox Jew could still
use the lift and not work (for operating a lift counts as work). 'But that is
ridiculous!,' the gentile exclaimed in rational indignation. 'Ah,' replied the
Jew. 'It is God's ridiculous ways that remind me that He is unknown.'

Although many Victorians struggled with the implications of the new
sciences for their beliefs, it was not until the twentieth century that
fundamentalism as a religious movement emerged and, more widely, that
words like conservative, orthodox, ultra-orthodox, Bible-believing,
traditionalist and infallibilist became virtually synonymous with
Christian, Islamic and Jewish commitment. It was in a similar timeframe
that modern militant atheism took hold as a cultural force, if a lesser one.

It is sometimes said that science gives rise to a world of 'two cultures' -
one is the culture of science and the other is the culture of art (or
perhaps religion). However, I believe that the polarisation is somewhat
different today. If my experience is anything to go by, and the analysis of
this chapter is right, then positions that might be thought of as on
opposite sides of the two cultures divide are actually just different
aspects of the same culture - the culture with a lust for certainty. This is
the reason why it is surprisingly easy to make the leap from belief to disbelief. It also lies behind the various forms of intellectual closure that
lurk in both atheistic and theistic discourse - a rejection of possibilities
both human and divine in favour of apparently sure grounds to stand
on. The question, then, is where the opposite of this culture of certainty
can be found, a worldview that embraces uncertainty, wise ignorance
and unknowing.

CHRISTIAN AGNOSTICISM: LEARNED IGNORANCE

He who reverently pursues the Boundless, even though he will never attain it, will himself advance by pushing forward in his pursuit.

St Hilary

THOMAS AQUINAS WAS KNOWN as the 'Dumb Ox' at school, probably on account of his substantial frame. He is second only to Augustine amongst heavyweight theologians, and was the lynchpin in the thirteenth-century embrace of Aristotle. His great achievement was the harmonisation of the writings of the ancient Greek - whose authority was such that he was referred to simply as 'The Philosopher' - with Christian thought. Thomas has been called a 'genius' in leading philosophy journals; 'one of the dozen greatest philosophers of the western world', by Anthony Kenny, one of his keenest contemporary readers; he was canonised by the Roman Catholic Church in 1323.

However, just 3 months before his death, something remarkable happened to this man of words. On 6 December 1273, he was celebrating the mass of the day, for St Nicholas, in the priory of San Domenico, Naples - where he was responsible for studies. The mass ended. But instead of continuing with his usual habit of calling for his secretary to continue writing, he stopped. From that moment on, he neither wrote nor dictated a single word again. The man whose intellect had grappled with the philosophy of nature, logic, metaphysics, morality, mind and theology was now silent.

It was not as if 6 December 1273 was a particularly good date upon which to put down his pen. His magnum opus, the *Summa Theologiae*, was far from complete in its Third Part. Modern biographers have put the abrupt halt down to a stroke or a breakdown caused by exhaustion. Others have said he had a mystical experience at the altar. But perhaps the truth of the matter is found in the response he gave to the colleague who begged him to continue: 'Reginald, I cannot, because all I have written seems like straw to me,' Thomas said.

The comment has been taken as a rejection of his oeuvre, from the master's own mouth, as if for 'straw' one should read 'rubbish'. But that would be to misunderstand what was said. Straw was, in fact, a conventional metaphor for a literal reading of the Bible. It expressed the conviction that a straightforward treatment of scripture might provide the believer with comfort, or some basic material upon which to build their faith, but that such a use of the Bible was only a first step. The implication of Thomas calling his work straw is therefore positive, not negative. His goal had been to understand God. He had made many attempts at the summit. But whilst they had produced wonderful insights - such as the reflections around the so-called proofs - he had reached the point at which he was able to appreciate the most profound truth of all. The peak lies beyond the clouds. God is unknown. Not in spite of, but because of, all his efforts - with its theological sophistication, subtlety and seriousness - the best interpretation of what happened to Thomas on St Nicholas's Day, 1273, was that he had reached as profound an appreciation of this mystery as was possible. Even his enquiries into how God is not would now stop. His new silence was not a rejection but the culmination of his life's work.

Move forward just over 800 years, to a seminar room in an Oxford college. Richard Swinburne, Emeritus Nolloth Professor of the Philosophy of the Christian Religion, is about to continue with the explication of his account of the existence of God. The session had begun well. One student, tape machine in hand, had asked whether he might record the seminar. 'There is no copyright on truth,' came the permission so to do. The hour proceeded in an orderly, if intellectually challenging, manner.

Until, that is, another student sat up in his chair. He had been reading a new book about the religious writings of the French philosopher

Jacques Derrida. His inquisitive mind had been particularly gripped by the idea summed up in the phrase 'religion without religion'. Derrida seemed to imply that any experience worth talking about - that is, a moment or an insight that was not merely hum-drum - has a religious character. This is because, for it to be such an experience, it must happen at the limits of what is possible. After all, is it not the case that the most amazing experiences of life are when what was thought impossible actually occurs? The book argued that this structure of experience, this 'becoming possible of the impossible', might even be a good definition of God. It was religious but without the usual trappings of religion. Perhaps, the student wondered, this might have a bearing upon Swinburne's argument about the existence of God.

He was wrong, or at least he soon got the message that he was wrong. For having explained the point, he received the abrupt response: 'I believe they offer a course on Derrida in the French department.' The seminar continued as before. That line of thought about God, on the becoming possible of the impossible, was curtailed - though not because of any inherent failures in it. Rather, it had simply been declared off-limits. The silence that the reprimand left in its wake was a negative one, not full of thought, but conspicuous by its emptiness.

These two anecdotes, the first famous in the history of medieval theology, the second mostly trivial though standing out as not atypical of half of my experience of studying theology at Oxford, illustrate two approaches to the subject. The former is an embrace of uncertainty. The latter aims to meet the demands of fact, application, veracity and coherence - the demands of *logos*. Thomas Aquinas, of course, was nothing if not rational: much of his work reads like logical puzzles and another of his titles could easily have been the Father of Scholasticism. However, he had the good fortune, theologically speaking, to live before the scientific worldview took hold. He understood that words, reason and argument must at some point give way before God, lest the divinity it discussed ceased to be God. His theology was a means to an end that it could not itself express. He could enter into a positive silence having exhausted all possibilities and sit with the impossible without shame or retribution. For many modern-day theologians, though, such a move is unspeakable - in the negative sense. Along with the atheists, the attempt to use words to throw the individual onto the unknowability of God is dismissed: different conservative religious parties would variously declare it 'continental', 'relativist', 'liberal' or 'heretical' (the atheist's preferred putdowns are 'incommensurate' or 'incoherent').

VARIETIES OF SILENCE

The story of Thomas opens up a whole new dimension to what Christianity has lost since the scientific revolution. In a word, silence. It is why someone can graduate with a degree in theology never having once written the word apophatic, and perhaps not even knowing what it is (God-talk by negation). It is why silence is such a rarity in churches. Modern services tend to kill it with two blows; first, by filling every minute with words - be they from the missal or the overhead projector; second, by making those words 'vernacular' - commonplace in language and meaning. It is why the ping-pong between conservative religionists and militant atheists will continue *ad infinitum* with nothing much new being said: neither can bear the thought that, if God exists, divinity ultimately lies beyond anything that can be said of it. Or to put it another way, God to be God must be heretical and inconsistent - beyond good and evil, and for that matter existence itself.

However, and this is Thomas's point, it is not simply true that nothing can be said about God. Everything possible, or at least a fair summary of everything that is possible, must be pursued before the move into silence.

This silence is of a certain sort: it is not empty but emptied; it is not a silence in which anything goes but in which nothing goes; it is not a place of resolved or dissolved argument but of irresolvable, indissoluble argument. Thomas was not silenced but he was drawn into silence, having spoken much. This kind of silence, then, requires much to be said because it must be the right kind of silence. It is a point at which someone arrives; their mind then 'moves upon silence' in W. B. Yeats's lovely phrase.

Needless to say, moving upon silence is not easy, perhaps suggesting again why it is a road less travelled. The notable exception to this is the Society of Friends or Quakers. However, Quaker silence is of a different sort to that of the Catholic Thomas. The central doctrine of the Quakers, as I understand it, is the 'Inner Light'. This is a sense of the divine, held collectively, that is superior to scriptures or doctrines. Meetings are conducted in silence from start to finish in order to facilitate discernment. Someone speaks when they feel stirred. All outward forms of worship are rejected as a hinderance to this discernment, this silence. Silence in the Catholic tradition works in the opposite way. Aesthetically rich liturgies draw the Christian into silence because God is beyond even the very best in words, images and music that the Church can offer. It is a silence of superfluity, not radical simplicity. The tried and tested way in the Christian tradition is to approach such silence by the way of negation. This *via negativa* is usually applied to God - to say what God is not. It offers a method for understanding something more about the nature of the silence itself too.

It is not, for example, the silence of the oppressed. The oppressed are silenced in order to crush their humanity. Their silence is neither voluntary, but is imposed by some power, nor does it represent the inexpressible, but rather it marginalises that which, politically speaking, should be expressed.

Neither is this religious silence like the inarticulacy of brute ignorance. The brute ignorant are silent about what they do not care about, not just about what they do not understand. Their silence is not humbled and considered, but is arrogant and thoughtless.

Another sort of silence that this religious silence can be distinguished from is the silence that is left when theology departs. This is the dangerous silence highlighted in the comment, widely attributed to G. K. Chesterton: 'When men stop believing in God they don't believe in nothing; they believe in anything.' In other words, there is, perhaps, a brief moment of metaphysical silence when people stop believing in God. But like nature and vacuums, people abhor *nihils*, and so struggle to fill the emptiness with something else - superstition and the like. (Incidentally, it is perhaps worth adding that I think this religious silence is not the same as the silence Wittgenstein famously refers to at the end of the *Tractatus Logico-Philosophicus*. His point is a specific one about philosophy, 'to say nothing accept what can be said' - with clarity and so on. What Wittgenstein's silence does is try to limit philosophy, narrow it down. For all the brilliance of other insights in the *Tractatus*, this dictum would seem to want to close philosophy off from all the 'big' questions that make it so gripping. Under this interpretation, his silence is a refusal, which religious silence is not.)

It is possible to speak more positively about religious silence too - using another theological method, this time of analogy. One example of a silence that has an awesome, religious quality is the silence associated with wonderment. We have considered this in relation to forming a critical but appreciative attitude towards science. And this wonderment can lead to silence too. At the time of writing, a capsule called Stardust had just returned to earth. The probe had travelled to a comet and back, a round trip of nearly 3 billion miles. At its rendezvous, in deep space 240 million miles from Earth, Stardust took photographs and grabbed some of the material from the comet nucleus. These particles, roughly one-hundredth the size of a printed full stop, have remained unchanged since the solar system formed 4.6 billion years ago. The whole trip took seven years.

Needless to say the scientists were tearful at the press conference, when announcing the mission's success. It was a truly remarkable feat of technology, vision and nerve. And one can talk about it as a purely human achievement, which it is. But there is, somehow, more going on too. This probe had ridden a small but impressive stretch of the vast empty seas of space, and returned to tell the tale. One could look at the potholed, charcoal grey casing of the capsule and glimpse indirectly what that otherwise inconceivable journey might be like. I watched it on the TV - in silence.

Religious silence might be said to be like the silence following the performance of a great piece of music too. After the final notes of a Mahler symphony, Bach's B minor mass, a Mozart opera or other great music, there is, sometimes, a brief pause. It is as if the audience and musicians hang together, indeterminate, like quantum particles, between the universe portrayed in the music and the world they normally inhabit. It is a moment that cannot last; a moment that collapses with the first 'Bravo!'. But it is one that can only be arrived at having been sated, even exhausted, by the music that preceded it.

It is perhaps also like the silence that is the mark of certain close friendships. It has been said that the measure of a good friendship is not how much or how often the friends speak, but how little the friendship demands they speak even though they are together for much of the time. They say they are comfortable in the silence. If friendship can be summed up as the desire to know someone and be known by them - as opposed, say, to erotic love which is the desire to have and be had by someone - then friendship will move towards a togetherness in silence as the friends come to a kind of knowing that is beyond words.

Another positive evocation of such silence comes from religious life, not the common or garden churchgoing variety, but the community variety of monks and nuns. At the end of every day, they say or sing the office of Compline, from the Latin *completorium* or complete. Literally, that refers to the completion of the offices for that day. However, each liturgical day also symbolically represents everything that can be said about God - in scripture, in psalmody, in creeds, in sacraments, in praise. So Compline also marks the point at which the monk or nun must turn to silence. This is literally the case too, since after Compline the so-called Greater Silence begins - the silence through the dark hours of the night. After the final part of Compline - the *Salve Regina*, the traditional Latin hymn before sleep - cowls are turned up, lights are turned off, and the community leaves the church in silence. From my experience of staying in religious houses for retreats, it is the most powerful moment of the day. The silence is thick with possibility. On the one hand, the office recognises that the night's silence may be full of 'fears and terrors', in the words of the office hymn - for sustained silence is a frightening thing. On the other hand, the silence portends the moment of death, the moment when words will cease forever. Compline powerfully conjures up another replete silence.

BEYOND EXPERIENCE

The apophatic tradition, also known as mystical theology, stresses a similar process of speaking in order to clear an intellectual path through what God is not to silence. In Christianity, one of the first great articulators of the unknowability of God was the fourth-century CE, Gregory of Nyssa. He argued that God was both infinite - lest God was limited by something - and unknowable, even in theory: after all, he says, echoing debates that continue to this day, we do not even know what the essence of an ant is, much less God.

Gregory taught that the inability to comprehend God forms the basis of a progress from the initial darkness of brute ignorance, through spiritual illumination, to a second darkness when the mind appreciates the mystery of God. He used the story of the encounters between God and Moses to illustrate the point. Before the Burning Bush, Moses was simply ignorant. The Burning Bush represents the phrase in which he tried to speak of God: for Moses, the high point of enunciation was in the revelation of the name of God - 'I am that I am' - though clearly, and quite deliberately, that phrase is no name. Next, Moses meets God in the pillar of cloud. This emphasises that, for all the light of his earlier theophany, God cannot actually be seen with the senses. Finally, on Mount Sinai, Moses learns that God cannot be known with the mind too. Divine darkness is the end of the journey that started with ignorant darkness.

Nicholas of Cusa, a fifteenth-century cardinal and forerunner of the Renaissance, fills out the parameters of this negative way. His best-known work was entitled *De docta ignorantia*, 'Of Learned Ignorance'. In it he pointed out that wise people from Solomon to Socrates realised that the most interesting things are difficult and unexplainable in words and that they know nothing except that they do not know. How, then, are we to interpret human beings' desire to know? The answer is that we desire to know that we do not know. This is the great challenge of the intellect:

If we can fully attain unto this [knowledge of our ignorance], we will attain unto learned ignorance. For a man - even one very well versed in learning - will attain unto nothing more perfect than to be found to be most learned in the ignorance which is distinctively his. The more he knows that he is unknowing, the more learned he will be.

In this learning, one learns something about what one does not know, as it were. Nicholas thought that truth was unitary, simple and absolute - and this was why it was unknowable: human beings know in ways that are multiple, complex and relative. The nature of human knowledge, therefore, is that it always results in contradictions. But it is in the *coincidentia oppositorum* - the realm in which all contradictions meet - that God dwells. Nicholas's book is full of mathematical examples, which he took to be the supreme science, to make the point - triangles that are

Illus. 5.1: The greatest challenge to the intellect, according to the fifteenth-century Socratic, Nicholas of Cusa, was what he called 'learned ignorance'.

circles at infinity, and so on. His words carry challenging implications for atheists and theists alike. For atheists, he makes the point that whatever they envisage God not to be, they must allow that image to be the most perfect thing possible. For theists, he emphasises that it is idolatrous to name God after created things, and that affirmative theology needs the sacred ignorance of negative theology to remember that God is ineffable. He concludes that strictly speaking God is neither known in this life nor in the life to come, since being infinity only infinity can comprehend itself. 'The precise truth shines incomprehensibly within the darkness of our ignorance' is a typically paradoxical formulation of his message.

Another apophatic theologian, Meister Eckhart, makes a point that is particularly prescient: the importance of drawing a clear line between silence and an experience of ecstasy. It is prescient because there is an emphasis on experiencing ecstasy in much contemporary churchgoing. This is Christianity that is authenticated by some kind of peak experience, from speaking in tongues, to being healed, to seeing a statue move. Typically, the experience is noisy, demonstrative and, *qua* the experience, often barely distinguishable from a bungee jump or druggy high. But this is Christianity as psychological buzz; its passion is no more than emotion. Its aims may be valid - happiness, satisfaction, belonging - but they eclipse the goal of spirituality, at least according to Eckhart, which is that of sacred ignorance.

For the pursuers of pure experience, the unknown is regarded suspiciously. They substitute the language of personal fulfilment for the language of vertiginous doubt. It is not going too far to say that Christianity as peak experience is the diametric opposite of what the great spiritual writers of the past meant when discussing the mystical life of the Christian (or indeed of other faiths). If anything they are notable for being against it: the whole point is to search for the God that is beyond experience, even esoteric experience. This is why they talk of 'divine darkness', 'emptiness' and 'mistrust of the senses'. In one sermon Meister Eckhart preached:

If thou lovest God as God, as spirit, as Person or as image, that must all go.

'Then how shall I love him?'

Love him as he is: a not-God, a non-spirit, a not-Person, a not-image; as sheer, pure, limpid unity, alien from all duality. And in this one let us sink down eternally from nothingness to nothingness.

He heaps up the impossibilities - a not-God, a non-spirit, a not-Person, a not-image - in order that God, spirit, Person, image might be left behind.

Here, then, is a tradition in which a strong, cultivated sense of uncertainty is the goal of its theology. It is characteristic of those who pursue it to premise everything they say on knowing that they do not know God. The aim is to hone the inability to speak of God so that things which are clearly wrong are discarded - which is to say, eventually, everything. The religiously minded agnostic will warm to all this for it is a way of doing God-talk that is simultaneously keen on the question of God but, contra much theism and atheism, insists that God is kept as a radical question. Little wonder that mystics like Eckhart frequently found themselves on the wrong side of the religious authorities.

If contemporary Christian practice has lost this core theological strand, then it seems to me that a serious, engaged agnosticism might be thought of as a check on the apparently unchecked use of positive statements about God - God's unqualified 'personhood' or 'fatherhood', and even lovingness and goodness. In other words, the reason for spending the last chapter critiquing theism and atheism is that it has brought us to the point at which an account of Christian-shaped agnosticism could begin. However, before continuing with that, there are two questions to answer that arise from the apophatic tradition. Although for apophatic theists God is unknown and unknowable, they can still say they are theists because they profess a Christian faith in God. The agnostic cannot readily say this. So the first question is: what is it that distinguishes the agnostic from the atheist, since, without the profession of a faith, it is not always clear how agnostic belief is distinguishable from atheistic belief? Second, and relatedly, if mystics state that God is unknown and unknowable, they do so having made a prior commitment in faith to divine reality. The agnostic is unsure of this reality, believing it is in the nature of God-talk not to be able to settle it. So does that not undermine the integrity of the agnostic position?

AGNOSTIC INTEGRITY

The first question was put into the mouth of Cleanthes by David Hume in his *Dialogues Concerning Natural Religion*. Cleanthes is the character who believes in natural theology. This is the attempt to gather insights about God from the world of nature and reason, on the good grounds that they are presumably both God's creation too. Cleanthes's charge is put to Demea, the character who is suspicious of what reason can achieve in theology because, for the divine to be divine, it must be beyond comprehension. He is not an agnostic though. He tends towards fideism, the belief in God by faith and faith alone. Cleanthes's complaint is that this is practically atheism since it allows nothing to be said about God's relationship with the world: 'How do you mystics,' he says, 'who maintain the absolute incomprehensibility of the Deity, differ from sceptics or atheists, who assert that the first cause of all is unknown and unintelligible?' Perhaps, they are atheists without knowing it.

I think our discussion so far provides answers to Cleanthes. For one thing, the atheist makes an assertion which the agnostic leaves as a question: the atheist says that God is not only not known or unintelligible, but is, further, not there. A second reason comes from something that all positions - theist, atheist and agnostic - can initially agree on, namely, that the world exists. As mentioned in the previous chapter, there are three response to this existence. The atheist says that existence is a problem that may or may not be explained, but ultimately it is just a fact. The theist may or may not say that existence can be explained, but they will say that ultimately it is a gift. The agnostic says that existence is not just a problem, but a mystery, for it can never be explained away. They may also regard it as a gift. So, in this way, once again, the agnostic differs from the atheist.

Thirdly, one can point to the different attitude that atheists and agnostics have to the mystics. For atheists, the apophatic is mostly gobbledegook. They may concede that some interesting insights about existential matters have been elicited by those operating on the margins of thought, but those gains to rationality are made at the unnecessary cost of an otherwise wilful obscurantism. For the agnostic, though, the apophatic not only has an integrity of its own but also is part of the valid search for ultimate things and, moreover, is an excellent embodiment of the Socratic wisdom of learned ignorance.

The second charge against the agnostic is more challenging. It is that they lack the prior commitment to faith in God, and so their apophaticism is, strictly speaking, pointless. The case can be fleshed out using another mystical theologian, Dionysius, also called the Pseudo-Areopagite. He makes the familiar moves implied by the inevitably slippery nature of theological language, moving through calling the reality beyond knowledge 'it', and even moving into the negation of negation, saying 'it is also beyond every denial'. His aim is to move his reader to a very profound silence indeed.

However, and this is where the challenge to the agnostic comes in, his multiple negations are made on the basis of a single affirmation: the negations negate the 'it'. Without that fixed point, Dionysius says, the force that drives the mystic into ever deeper contradictions becomes unstable, and the specificity of the apophatic silence disintegrates into unfocussed intellectual turbulence. He uses the analogy of the sculptor, searching for the 'pure view of the hidden image' inside the stone or wood. The accusation is that the agnostic will obliterate the hidden image like a bad sculptor who removes too much.

This difference is, I think, substantial. It turns on the fact that the agnostic does not adhere to a particular faith; the believer does. Even if the believer's exploration of God reduces all that can be said to an 'it', and then negates that since an 'it' implies an object which God is not, faith allows the believer to affirm the 'it' knowing it is provisional, which the agnostic, unequivocally, cannot. The question, then, is whether there is a difference between the agnostic and the believer that disqualifies the agnostic's mysticism without faith?

Anthony Kenny has written about how both can still share the silence in relation to the poet Arthur Hugh Clough. Clough was a contemporary, colleague and correspondent of Matthew Arnold, the poet famous for 'Dover Beach', with its metaphor of the 'withdrawing roar' of the 'Sea of Faith'. Kenny shows how, of the two agnostics, Clough captures the ineffability of God more precisely, and in so doing provides an example of a genuine agnostic apophaticism.

Kenny considers Clough's poem *humnos haumnos* (a hymn, yet not a hymn) in a collection of his essays entitled *The Unknown God*. The poem begins by addressing the divine who dwells in human shrines, though immediately notes that this image of God 'Doth vanish, part, and leave behind / mere blank and void of empty mind'. The second stanza articulates the mystic's conundrum, of speaking about the unknown, and confesses that, 'The imperfect utterance fell unmade.' In the third stanza the more radical turn is taken, of negating even the negations. 'I will not frame one thought of what / Thou mayest either be or not.' The poet cannot only not say 'thus and so', but neither 'no' too.

Then, in the fourth stanza, Clough distances himself from the believer who, although similarly mystic, might have faith to receive a revelation beyond human words: 'I will not ask some upper air,' the agnostic says. What is left? If the agnostic must admit that they cannot turn to faith, what shape can their agnosticism take? Oddly, it is a prayer:

> Do only thou in that dim shrine,
> Unknown or known, remain, divine;
> There, or if not, at least in eyes
> That scan the fact that round them lies.
> The hand to sway, the judgement guide,
> In sight and sense, thyself divide:
> Be thou but there - in soul and heart,
> I will not ask to feel thou art.

The poet has reached a point of being reconciled with the fact that they cannot make the minimal, Dionysian affirmation of the 'it'. The question of God is suspended, 'unknown or known'. Perhaps this God is only in the minds of those who 'scan' the world around them. However, even so, the final stanza concludes on this surprisingly prayerful note. The poet ends by seeking divine guidance and discernment 'in sight and sense' nonetheless. How can this be? Does this not require some positive sense that God is? Does not someone who makes such a prayer need to ask 'to feel thou art'? Kenny writes:

> No, the prayer need not assume the truth of that; only its *possibility* is needed. An agnostic's praying to a God whose existence he doubts is no more unreasonable than the act of a man adrift in the

ocean, or stranded on a mountainside, who cries for help though he may never be heard, or fires a signal which may never be seen. Of course the need for help need not be the only motive which may drive an agnostic to prayer: the desire to give thanks for the beauty and wonder of the world may be another.

It is Kenny's last comment that saves the *via negativa* for the agnostic, that preserves a sense of radically unknowing silence with integrity. Like thorough-going uncertainty which regards existence as a mystery and therefore maintains the possibility that it is gift, the possibility that God 'is' is the minimal requirement which keeps the search via learned ignorance from spinning out of control. That possibility means that the agnostic can return to the things that are said about God, and their negations. It is only if God ceases to be regarded as a possibility that can be treated seriously that the apophatic quest loses its *raison d'être*.

If it is perfectly valid for Clough's poem to end in prayer, of a particularly purged sort, there is another sense in which it is not only an appropriate but a necessary end. What it emphasises is that the *via negativa* is an ongoing process. Remember that the poem begins with an invocation of God - 'O Thou'. The prayer at the end requires a return to the beginning; in calling out again to that now dimmer 'shrine', the poet repeats the process of unknowing. This is not because the agnostic is condemned to some pitiful attempt to call out to a deity who is really not there. Rather, the prayer for divine guidance and discernment requires it. Like repeatedly reading a wonderful novel, or hearing great music time and time again, each repetition changes and deepens one's relationship with the process of negation. This is, in Eckhart's phrase, a sinking 'down eternally from nothingness to nothingness'.

How may one try to think about this, for clearly it is a process ultimately as indescribable as the non-image of God it seeks? Well, there is a parallel in the process of Socratic philosophy. Socrates' insight was that wisdom is found in a knowledge of ignorance. Such wisdom is not arrived at simply by admitting that one is ignorant; that is not enough. One must explore the nature of one's ignorance as deeply as possible. Like mystical prayer, it is to this extent a process of unknowing. This is why Socrates did not stand in the agora simply preaching a message of condemnation to his fellow Athenians for their unacknowledged ignorance, but he engaged them, to discover more about his ignorance and theirs. In this way, he nurtured a way of life that came to be called philosophy. Similarly, mysticism is not simply an assertion that, whatever else the divine might be, divinity is unknown. Rather, it has as its goal an ever more profound appreciation of this truth. The cycle of invocation, negation, invocation, negation, that Clough's poem sets up is, therefore, the fundamental pattern of the mystical life. Replace 'invocation' with 'question', and one has the pattern of the Socratic life too - question, negation, question, negation.

The paradox is that this is often a highly rational process. This is partly why to read Eckhart or Dionysius or Nicholas of Cusa or Anselm is to find a remarkably similar tone to some passages in Plato's dialogues. Plato does not give thanks to Christ, of course, and the Christian theologians do not flirt with Athenian youths. Also one should remember that the Christian mystics read Plato or neo-Platonists so my observation is slightly circular. However, it is for good reason that both genres of writing play with the ambiguities of verbs like 'to be' or 'to love'. It is for good reason that in both there is a sense of identifying errors in order to establish a clearer way forward; that both use mathematical analogies and logical conundrums; that both allude to theophanies beyond words; that both admit of no final resolution. Such as they are, these similarities are an encouragement and a challenge. The encouragement is what one might call the demystification of mystery: the aim is not to nurture some esoteric experience, like a wannabe Buddha struggling to emulate higher levels of meditation; the mystical path is no more, or less, opaque than philosophy. The challenge is that learning ignorance is at least as hard as Socratic philosophy!

THE PROBLEM OF EVIL

There is more to say on the similarities and differences of agnostics and believers, and even more on the sense in which philosophy may, in a certain sense, be agnostic and religious. However, first, I want to suggest another path into silence that also tackles an issue that is for many perhaps the greatest barrier to belief - namely, the problem of evil.

The problem of evil is the problem of how a good, loving, all-knowing, all-powerful God could allow suffering in a world of that same God's creation. Should not divine goodness require, divine love desire, divine omniscience understand, and divine omnipotence enable a world in which suffering was not necessary? The problem finds one of its most forceful modern articulations in Dostoevsky. One of the Karamazov brothers, Ivan, complains to his brother Alyosha, that he cannot understand how the world will ever find the harmony, promised in religion, of a divinely ordained reconciliation of evil with good. He takes the extreme case of a tortured child. He knows that God's ways are way beyond the power of human understanding, but he simply cannot conceive of a moment when he could forgive the torturer of such a child. He runs through various arguments that are put to dissolve the problem. A philosopher might intellectually sidestep the issue by saying that the problem of suffering is really a subset of the problem of how someone can know of another's experience. A humanitarian might say that the problem of evil must be resolved in forgiveness of even the most heinous crimes, for only then can suffering stop. But Ivan resists such 'solutions'. Even if the child forgave the torturer - even if the child's mother forgave him - the tears of the child would remain spilt, screaming out for atonement. He cannot help but feel that creation is not worth it, if it costs the suffering of that child.

Various other answers are offered to the problem of evil. Another philosopher might say that evil is necessary if human beings are to be moral and free. The argument here is that the corollary of a world without evil is a world in which everything people did would automatically be good. This, though, would mean we could not make moral choices - something that would lessen our humanity and make us little more than virtuous robots. Similarly, if someone else argued that any divinity worth its salt should intervene to save people from suffering, the implication would be that there were no consequences of human beings doing evil, since God would prevent it. This would morally infantilise us.

But for all these apparently unassailable arguments, the suffering, the evil and the revulsion of what happened to that child remain. The problem persists, as does the hurdle it represents for belief in God. This is arguably one message of the book of Job in the Bible, the story of the man who suffered foul calamities and foul disease, apparently at the behest of God. Although God gains some credit at the end of the book for chastising Job's tormentors - his 'friends' who tell him his suffering must have some 'meaning' as punishment - God comes out of the story as a monster who followed Satan's agenda, the angel whose challenge to God initiates Job's tragedy. The book of Job seems to say that it is better to think God a monster than to think the problem of evil can be solved and that suffering need no longer be a concern.

To put it another way, the most valid response to suffering, whatever the content of that response, is not via abstract argument but is in real experience. After all, the irreducibility of evil stems from its ever tangible presence. Cautiously, then, for to write about the problem of evil is always to risk complacency, I would offer two reflections, one from my own experience, one from experiencing a tragedy faced by others.

My own experience is that of the early death of my mother. The bare facts are familiar ones. She had cancer and, after various treatments and the roller-coaster ride of hope and dismay, the disease became terminal. Medical science gained us two years whilst she was ill, and they were invaluable: as has been observed before, mortality, when one is conscious of its irresistibility, comes with the strange gift of living life in all its fulness. I understood the wisdom of the ancient liturgy which asks to be saved from sudden death. Then, though, my mother died. I remember the shivery sigh of her last exhalation and the waxy texture of her skin as I kissed goodbye.

At the funeral, which was a requiem mass, I did not receive communion. This was partly because I was at the time still an atheist. I could appreciate the value of the ceremony as a rite of passage, and that kneeling to receive the bread and wine might be a very good way of admitting my vulnerability at her death - especially since it would be to do so with others who also mourned her loss. However, in my mind, this benefit was outweighed by also needing to express my conviction that the world was godless. At that moment in time, that seemed to be the best response to her too early death. It was not that I felt angry, just the need to be quietly resolute in the implications of my atheistic belief.

In the period after her death, though, my mind changed. What I had not expected was the way my 'dead' mother was present to me for

Illus. 5.2: It is better to think that God is a monster than that the problem of evil can be solved - the message of Job?

months, and then years. For a long time, I was very conscious of what she might have said or felt in a particular moment. Some people who lose someone close, like a lover, find themselves talking to the person who has died, and eventually find a kind of happiness in doing so. This was not so for me. Instead, I had dreams in which my mother lived on, though in a kind of parallel universe. I would recognise her but also recognise she was becoming different. What this made me realise is that I would not get over her death; it would always be with me in some shape or form. However, I would learn to live with it and even, possibly, live a little better because of it - a little more conscious of my own mortality, a little more attentive to the present moment.

The question became how to *do* this new way of living as well as possible? I did not want to 'get closure', as the ugly phrase from pop-psychology has it. Even if closure were doable, it would be to move on, not live with. Neither did I want the comforts of the language of immortality for it did not feel right to simply say that my mother was in heaven or just on the other side of the veil. If pushed, even now I tend to think that I won't see her again because identity without a body is inconceivable and her body has most certainly gone. However, I also had this spiritual sense in which she has not straightforwardly 'gone' either.

An uncertain though nonetheless Christian-shaped response has proven to be the answer. As I lost my atheism, and my religious imagination returned, it was the silence of certain liturgies that came to shape the ambivalence of, on the one hand, the clarity of my remembrance and, on the other, the lack of clarity as to what death may or may not be. One such service is the ashing of Ash Wednesday. Here, the priest marks the penitent on the forehead with the sign of the cross, saying, 'Remember you are dust and to dust you shall return.' The stark reality of that act is chastening, of course, and to some might be objectionable. But it is an intimate moment: the ashing becomes an oddly life affirming assertion of one's mortality.

Another service that I found capturing my ambivalence was All Souls Day, when churches of a catholic persuasion have a requiem mass at which the dead are remembered by name. I now look out for a service that includes a liturgical performance of one of the great Requiem Masses. Several composers have written some of their most profound music in response to this rite, capturing the mixed uncertainties of death, loss, aspiration and hope. Though the All Souls Mass is full of words and sound, its purpose makes it different from other services. It becomes a container for an underlying silence which I now take to be the best response to my mother's death. Christianity has become for me, in this context at least and to use Denis Potter's phrase, 'the wound, not a bandage'.

What this has to do with the more general problem of evil is to suggest that, having been exposed to some manifestation of it and all that it implies, a final response of silence represents not its resolution but its fullest expression. Like a *via negativa*, the problem of evil provokes multiple objections, such as the sense of injustice, anger and horror. To these, part-solutions can be suggested. But, always, the problem of evil remains, its resolution unknown. I am not saying that suffering is redeemed if something is learnt from it, as if the suffering itself might be thought good. It is irreducible. Rather, it is that suffering may be an occasion for unlearning certain things that are otherwise taken for granted, notably the illusion of immortality. This may, in turn, be best expressed in a religiously shaped silence that emerges as the questions are wrestled with. In other words, theodicy - the confrontation with the problem of evil - can become another path into unknowing.

Someone might object that this is all very well at a personal level. It is, after all, my responsibility and right to respond to my mother's death as I choose. But what of the objective sense of injustice within the problem of evil - Ivan Karamazov's point that the sufferings of a child for the sake of creation will call out for all eternity? Again, this is a genuine sticking point that ultimately admits of no dissolution. Given that, the question becomes how to live with the impasse?

The tsunami disaster of Boxing Day 2004 is a salient event here. Witnessing this, and asking the fundamental question, 'Where was God?', offers another reflection on theodicy. Several things struck me. In the West, the disaster provoked prominent atheists to rehearse the argument for the non-existence of God. They echoed Voltaire who wrote similarly following the Lisbon earthquake of 1755. 'This is indeed a cruel piece of natural philosophy!' he cried. 'What a game of chance human life is!' It should crush the sanctimonious, he continued, for it is the mountains of human achievement that will save people from earth-quakes, if anything.

However, two things stuck out in the aftermath of the tsunami which make that humanist outrage inadequate, if understandable. One was the way in which the people involved turned to religion as a response to their often terrible loss. To deploy the metaphor of the wound and bandages again, the material superiority of the Western world could and did provide the means to fly absolutely necessary aid into the disaster zones - that is, to provide the bandages. However, when it came to seeking means of expressing just what it was that the tsunami had inflicted - the nature of the wound - it was religion that people turned to. Although some people were wholly understandably angry with God, there appeared to be no objections to Buddhist monks chant-ing on beaches in Thailand, mosques becoming places of refuge in Indonesia, and Hindi prayers being offered in Sri Lanka. Indeed, they were wanted. Bernard Williams, the philosopher, was once con-fronted with the objection that religious faith might be thought of as colluding with a God who allows bad things to happen. He replied that such a position overlooks what religion does for people. 'That religion can be a nasty business', he wrote, 'is a fact built into any religion worth wor-rying about, and that is one reason why it has seemed to so many people the only adequate response to the nasty business that everything is.'

This turn to God is unnerving to the secular mind. In fact, in all hon-esty, it is unnerving to the Western religious mind too since it seems to lack the resentment that is the natural response in those who have come to believe that it is almost a right not to have to suffer. Materialism can patch things up, but reading of people being able to get on with life in the face of terrible events is quite as shocking as the mother in Dostoevsky who can forgive the torturer of her child. As it happened, I was in Thailand during the spring of 2005, a few months after the tsunami, albeit in a coastal area that was not as badly damaged by the wave as some. I did indeed find that silence was the only final response after asking and hearing about what had happened.

I have been advocating silence. It is silence of a particular sort, since it only comes after everything has been said about the problem in hand - be that the question of God, or the problem of evil. Being thrown into silence in this way is a profoundly agnostic process. It stems from the radical unknowability of God, and the requirement to learn and relearn ignorance of the divine - the great insight of the mystics. Of course, believers - in my context - are the chief guardians of this tradition, since they preserve the writings, liturgies and ways of life that embody it. Which is to say that the Christian agnostic needs the Christian believer: it is, after all, hard to imagine a world of only Christian agnostics in which prayer would last, let alone flourish. However, there is also a sense in which the believer needs the agnostic. The religiously minded but deliberately undecided agnostic can ensure that the central affirmation of the faith is not reified. If, as I have argued, much Christian practice today cannot stomach this uncertainty, because it is antithetical to the desire for an orthodoxy that can supply spiritual certainties and peak experience, the religious-minded agnostic has a particular role to play. Paradoxically, it is their committed uncertainty that might revivify the first and last commitments of the religious quest: God is unknown because divine.

WAGERING ON GOD

The truth of this lies behind another argument that is frequently rehearsed in debates between theists and atheists - namely, Pascal's so-called wager. Like the proofs of God, it is routinely misunderstood.

The wager is usually taken to be something like as follows. If God does not exist then, upon death, the individual will know nothing of it. If God does exist then, upon death, the individual will know it for a fact. Moreover, if they believed in God, the benefits that come with faith will then be visited upon them. So, it is better to act as if God does exist, and believe, than to act as if God does not. The problem for the wager when presented like this is that it makes faith out to be not only a calculation, but calculated - an objectionable quality that undermines the value of faith.

That, though, is a gross misrepresentation of Pascal. The first point to note is that he was a believer (of a particularly conservative sort). Like Anselm, his reflections only make sense when that is borne in mind. In the *Pensées*, in which the wager text is found, he is grappling with the unavoidable antinomies of his faith - unavoidable because of the nature

of God. In particular it is the undecidability of God's existence -
because God is beyond human comprehension, and certainly beyond the
powers of human reason to prove - that interests him. What then can
reason say of believing, or not, in God?

He thinks that faith, if not founded on reason, should, nonetheless,
be as rationally justified as possible. This is where the wager comes in.
What he argues is that the position of believing in God makes more
sense than the position of not believing in God, since although both
positions are adopted in the face of an uncertainty that reason cannot
overcome, the believer in God wins an infinite prize. His argument,
then, is aimed not at converting the atheist but rather at the lesser task
of calling their rational certainties into question which includes the
assumption that theism is less rational than atheism. Using mathematical probability theory, which he takes to be something both he and his
opponent would agree is sufficient for good reasoning, though clearly
not for good belief, he hopes to unsettle the atheist.

The argument has other benefits for it allows Pascal to make some
interesting observations. For example, if the sceptic is worried that confessing a belief in God would be to compromise his rational powers, he
is worrying about the wrong thing: reason alone cannot decide one way
or the other. In fact, I suspect that admitting this was as much a blow
for Pascal as it might be for the atheist. Probably the most famous quote
from this section, and the whole of the *Pensées*, is: 'The heart has its reasons which reason itself does not know'. As it happens, Pascal wrote this
upside-down and in a margin. This is, I think, significant. It seems to be
a sign of despair stemming from a keen insight: it is as if he were saying,
'for all that I can reason about my faith, ultimately my reason cannot get
to the crux of it. That comes from my heart, the organ of an altogether
different kind of knowledge.' (He continues the famous sentence with
the far less poetic clause 'we know that through countless things', suggesting again that he did not think he was crafting a memorable apho-
rism, merely making a blunt observation.)

In other words, in spite of the force of Pascal's argument, he is also
forced to remind himself that reason is barely a start. Like the rudder of
a ship, it may point the boat in the right direction, but it is the wind of
faith that fills the sails and propels the believer forward. To wager on

God is therefore to do something necessary but minimal: it is to do no more or less than take the stance that talking about God is worth it. At the very least it is not unreasonable to do so; at most there is, possibly, everything to gain. Implicitly, then, the argument also gives support to the reasonableness of the agnostic position.

THE CHARGE OF DEISM

Having said that, Pascal would have had no truck with agnosticism. His wager might cohere with the agnostic stance but, he would argue, it is no more a reason for remaining uncertain than it is a reason for believing or not believing - it is not a sufficient reason for anything. What the agnostic is accused of is what he accuses the atheist of too. It is not reason that stops you believing, Pascal says, since there is no good reason not too. Rather it is your passion - that complex of personal temperament, history and obstinacy. The charge is that the agnostic, and the atheist, do not allow their hearts to speak to them; Pascal might agree that it would be nice if reason could decide, but, given that it cannot, that is no reason to block out one's feelings.

We have a clear indicator of what Pascal's feelings told him. On the night of 23 November 1654, the feast of Saint Clement, he had a vision. 'From about half past ten in the evening until about half past midnight. Fire,' he wrote on a piece of paper, now known as 'The Memorial'. He subsequently sewed it into his clothes. In what followed these first phrases he articulated a distinction that mirrors the role of reason and feeling in matters of religion. The distinction is between the God of the 'philosophers and scholars' and the 'God of Abraham, God of Isaac, God of Jacob'. The implication is that the former divinity does not live, whereas the latter God does. One can easily imagine that for Pascal, far from being the beginning and end of religion, apophaticism is only a prolegomenon to faith. After all, no-one could worship the deity of the philosophers. It is the God loved by the community of faith that is worth seeking.

Pascal's implicit accusation is that of deism - the belief that God can only be known through reason not revelation. Pascal can be taken as saying that the agnostic might be open to God-talk but is not open to the ways in which God might actually talk to us!

The charge is serious. Is it not reasonable to assume that if there is a God, that God would make himself known to us, one way or another? Doubly so if God is a God of love. For what is the point of a God who may have written the rules of nature, and even given the universe its first nudge as those rules kicked in, to be subsequently effectively absent. As T. H. Huxley powerfully observed:

> Whether astronomy and geology can or cannot be made to agree with the statements as to matters of faith laid down in Genesis - whether the Gospels are historically true or not - are matters of comparatively small moment in the face of the impassable gulf between the anthropomorphisms (however refined) of theology and the passionless impersonality of the unknown and unknow-able which science shows everywhere underlying the thin veil of phenomenon.

There are several things to say about this. First, the agnostic position I am exploring is not denying that people might feel that God speaks to them, or that God is revealed through processes of scripture, incarnation and prayer. Indeed, inasmuch as it is serious about engaging with religious traditions, it pays attention to them. However, for a complex of reason and feeling, the agnostic does so without the certainties of faith. Probably the most powerful argument for adhering to this position, which is another version of Huxley's 'impassable gulf', is that even if God did want to make himself known that would have to happen within the limits of human understanding. So whatever it might be that would signify that this 'making known' was divine it would be lost in its reception. How could one know this communication was of God and not of the human imagination? Such is our predicament.

Where I think Huxley goes too far is in suggesting that this casts the agnostic adrift in a cold sea of unknowing. There is another distinction to draw here. Although the divine is unknown in itself - even to the extent of its existence - that is not to say that we can know nothing *about* divinity, as concept and perhaps as reality. Whatever God might be, we can say what God is not. Trivially, for example, we can say that God is not, say, the golden calf that my neighbour may erect in their back garden to fall down and worship. More interestingly, we can say that God is not the idea of the divinity presented by many atheists, or indeed theists. This is the whole point of the apophatic tradition, the negations and then negation of negations, that not only can be said of God but must be said in any decent theology. God-talk is not empty; the silence is full.

For the same reason, the agnostic stance need not be deist. There is nothing in agnosticism that relegates God to the margins of creation - its beginning and, if it has one, its end. In fact, I suspect that idea is itself mistaken. If the fundamental mystery in life is existence itself, why there is something rather than nothing, *and* one does not have the belief of the atheist, that existence itself is just brute fact, then the quest for God is potentially provoked every waking moment of the day. One might go so far as to say an agnostic could not be a deist, for deism is a positive belief about God.

Rather agnosticism manifests itself best as an attitude. It is a way of life driven by the desire for ultimate things. It is a love in the way that philosophy was a love of wisdom for Socrates. It is a 'passionate commitment' to a certain form of life, in Wittgenstein's phrase. What marks it out is a confession of ignorance - a confession both in the sense of an admittance and in the sense of a framework.

Following Socrates: a Way of Life

It was modesty that invented the word 'philosopher' in Greece.

Nietzsche

ST PAUL IS LOCKED UP in a dank Roman dungeon with St Peter, on the night before their executions. It is a predicament that focusses the mind and elicits honesty. Peter, in particular, has a confession to make. He knows that what he must say to Paul could be shattering. After a few false starts and circumlocutions, he gets to the point. He tells Paul that Jesus did not rise again. He was resuscitated. On that fateful Friday, years before, Jesus did not have time to die the slow death of crucifixion with the Sabbath starting only hours after he was hung from the tree. Worse still, the Jesus Paul had seen on the road to Tarsus was not a vision: he was the real thing. After the trauma of the torture, Jesus had become obsessed with Paul who before his conversion was second to none in persecuting Jesus' followers. It was pure coincidence that their paths had crossed - affording Jesus the chance to ask Paul why himself. What had doubly shocked Jesus, his brother James and Peter, though, was the subsequent turn of events. They had thought Jesus' message was for the Jews alone. They did not suppose that Paul would join them, and then take the gospel half way around the world!

This is the version of events told in the recent play *Paul* by Howard Brenton. And it might be thought controversial. That it did not attract much animosity, at least when it was on at the National Theatre in London in 2005, might have been because people saw that it would be wrong to take it as yet another historicist attack on the Christian story. Brenton's point is far more subtle than that. For what happens after Peter makes his confession to Paul is not what Peter had feared. Paul is not crushed by the revelation. He does not take it to mean that his life's work has been in vain. Why? Because regardless of the facts, he knows that his encounter with this man Jesus changed him. Now, years on, even an apparently devastating exposé of what actually happened cannot undo that. This is the reality that is most immediate to him. Christianity had become for him a way of life, one that was powerfully transforming. In the closing scene of the play, the two apostles hold each other and prepare for the moment that they had long known their way of life would bring them to - the time to die.

What I take the play to be highlighting is the thing about faith that bemuses the scientific mind above all else. Religion is not just a set of beliefs or a moral code. It is a way of seeing the world and a way of shaping existence. This is why it is so resistant to being questioned and mocked, why attacks with reason and ridicule are as likely to sustain it as undermine it. The scientific revolution may have undermined mythical ways of understanding. But whilst making religion forgetful of the unknowability of God, and aggressive towards its despisers, it still thrives because it is a thing of the heart and of the head; it is not done in abstract but in lives.

This also explains the reason why, although I lost my faith, I found atheism unsatisfying. Atheism is not a practice but a principle. It may be supplemented, as it were, by the arts, ethical causes or a strong commitment to a rationalist, empirical view of life. But in secular guise at least, these ways of life are wary of the soul. My religious imagination demanded something else. But as an agnostic, is that any more nourishing of a life? One might be persuaded that science oversteps its limits and that a wonderment that nurtures value, connection and piety is essential for the recovery of a more humble approach. One might also accept that something has gone wrong with modern religion in its forgetfulness of the unknowability of God and the centrality of silence. For what it's worth, scepticism about science, the romantic appreciation of nature, scholastic mystical theology and the silencing power of theodicy are all premised on an agnosticism that has enabled me to move beyond atheism. This is the power of its critique. However, for life, one must move from the deconstructive to the constructive, from merely seeing the world in a certain way to shaping existence into a way of life. If agnosticism cannot do that then it will never be much more than a shrug of the shoulders. Does it add up to a commitment and an ethos? Can it too be a way of life?

My suggestion is yes, and that agnosticism as a way of life rests on the shoulders of Socrates. It is not uncommon for thinkers to turn to Socrates for inspiration in this way. Philosophers as diverse as Hegel and Nietzsche, Kierkegaard and Montaigne have done so; as Cicero put it: 'Socrates was the first to call philosophy down from the heavens and compel it to ask questions about life and morality.' He is often associated with scepticism on account of his *modus operandi* - namely, inquiry. The agnosticism that I want to associate him with is scepticism of a particular sort. It is not like some forms of modern scepticism that are mostly intellectual in scope: Socrates was not solipsistic, for example, as if he thought he might be only a 'brain in a vat'. As I see it, he was not sceptical about the existence of things, nor the power of reason, nor crucially about the value of life. Quite the reverse.

He was sceptical about what human beings can know for sure, on account of their in-between status between the animals and the gods. This is both a burden, inasmuch as the individual can become conscious of their ignorance. But it is also a blessing. Socrates' agnosticism meant that whilst using reason to understand the nature of his ignorance more fully, he also knew that reason alone was not enough; it too has its limits - most notably when it comes to matters theological. So Socratic philosophy did not stop at the point at which reason could go no further. Rather, it was but part of a philosophical way of life - the life we can still catch a glimpse of in the person of the historical Socrates. It is this that makes me think that Socratic agnosticism carries the seeds of an ethos as well as the principles of an intellectual exercise, a practice that can embrace the whole of life as well as an approach that can engage the mind. The question is how and what does that life, after Socrates, look like?

Plato is the starting point. This is partly for the obvious reason that he is the best source of our knowledge of Socrates. But, more importantly, Plato's encounter with Socrates led him to forge a way of life that included writing about Socrates in such a way as to instil the same imperative in his readers. He presents Socrates to us in such a way as to nurture an ethos as well as provide an education.

ENCOUNTERING SOCRATES

Not much is known about Plato's life before his encounter with the gad-fly of Athens. He was from an aristocratic, politically active family, and it is likely that his turn to full-time philosophy came after disillusion-ment with politics - perhaps as a result of having seen Socrates con-demned at the hand of a democratic state. He may have been a wrestler in his youth, if you believe the speculation that his name was actually a pun on the Greek for 'broad' - *platus* - as in 'broad-shouldered'. He may have travelled in Egypt in his early life, seeking wisdom in what was an ancient culture even to the ancient Greeks. He did not marry. Any indications as to his character are tentative since, apart possibly from the so-called *Seventh Letter*, he wrote nothing in his own voice.

But after they met, everything changed. The influence of Socrates on him was massive and profound. It has been called fateful, because after-wards life never looked the same again. There is a story that on the day Plato met Socrates he was due to have a tragedy performed in the the-atre of Dionysos, the Theatre Royal of Athens. Plato cancelled the per-formance and burnt the manuscript there and then. Socrates made Plato re-examine everything: this is why Socrates is always depicted in the dialogues as on the move, questioning, seeking truth. And this is what made Plato wiser, not that Socrates revealed doctrines to him, but that Socrates' passionate desire for what was good and true, his love of wis-dom, captivated Plato too. After all, what is it that makes a person truly wise? Not, actually, that they utter sagacious words, even less that they know it all. Neither is it that they are warm or welcoming, for to meet them might be unsettling. Rather, their wisdom is manifest in their attitude, in the sense that they are digging deep. Their wisdom is appealing because, being with them, you are enabled to dig deeper too - the work of a committed agnostic.

What was a momentous meeting for Plato could have become just a paragraph in the history of philosophy, and no more important than a detail like knowing that Kant read Hume or that Wittgenstein argued with Popper. That it is far more important than either of those facts is not just because Socrates features in nearly every Platonic dialogue. It is because Plato constructs them in such a way as to conjure up something of the same sense of encounter with Socrates in us, his readers.

He does this partly by his inclusion of descriptions of Socrates' impact on those around him. 'I made progress when I was with you, if only in the same house, not even in the same room; and still more, so it seemed to me, when I was in the same room and looked at you (rather than elsewhere) while you were talking; but most of all when I sat beside you, quite close, and touched you,' says one of Plato's characters, Aristeides.

It is also implicit in the way the dialogues are constructed. For example, many have rather tortuous introductions: the *Symposium* begins with one Apollodorus addressing anonymous individuals who are asking about what happened at the famous drinking party. The anonymous individuals are us - reading to find out the same thing. Moreover, 'we', as it were, are not the first to ask Apollodorus this question. Another, Glaucon, has recently asked him the same thing too. And, as if to underline the point again, Apollodorus himself says that he only knows about the occasion secondhand. Luckily for him, and us, he managed to glean the details from Aristodemus. In this way, Plato identifies his readers with his characters: we are encouraged to see ourselves, personally as well as intellectually, drawn to the action too.

Other devices Plato uses throw the content of the dialogues onto his readers, forcing them to make it their own. The early dialogues in particular are characterised by ending in agnostic impasses - *aporia*: 'We think we are friends but just what friendship is we have not been able to discover,' Socrates says at the end of the *Lysis*, inviting the reader to think more on the issue and on their own experience of friendship. For some readers, the uncertainty that *aporia* implies is unnerving, even unwanted, because nothing conclusive is ever reached. But as well as accurately reflecting Socrates' conviction that he knew nothing for sure, and that there is therefore always more to be said - more to be lived - an *aporia* is also a cunning literary device, ensuring the dialogues can never be treated as philosophical treatises that might be thought to wrap things up. They raise questions that only the reader can answer for themselves.

Socrates is also often ironic in the dialogues, particularly when it comes to confessing his ignorance. Not that he secretly thinks he *does* know about things! It was just that inevitably, after a while, he reached a point when the common mistakes that people make in deluding themselves that they know more than they do became familiar to him. And since his goal was to encourage them to understand their ignornace, rather than just tell them about it, he has to go along with them to tease it out. Like an old teacher in front of a new class, he pretends that their queries, difficulties, enthusiasms and conclusions are as fresh to him as they are to them. Sometimes, his bluff is called: 'You have gone too far this time,' Agathon says in the *Symposium* when Socrates repeats again that he is ignorant on such and such a matter. But he insists: he is genuine in his confession. (Irony is also a good strategy for stirring arrogant people up: it irritates them by pricking bubbles.)

More positively, at its best, Socratic philosophy is a form of friendship. Partly because both are nothing if not lived. And partly because the best kinds of friends are those who make the best kind of philosopher. They are people who know each other, can speak freely with each other, are honest and humble towards one another, and can critique and challenge each other. In the dialogues, Socrates has his most rewarding conversations with individuals who can accept friendship of this sort (and conversely, those that cannot are the least productive). To borrow from Emerson, Socratic friends are like those who exclaim, 'Do you see the same truth!'

Finally, the most obvious underlining of the belief that it is a sense of encounter that Plato is trying to conjure up is that Plato wrote in dialogues in the first place. The *Seventh Letter* suggests that Plato resisted writing anything at all for a time, since he feared it would detract from what he really thought philosophy was - something done in life. Thankfully for us, he was persuaded apparently because it would enable him to reach a wider audience. The dialogue was his answer to the necessary compromise because if writing is not the real thing at least dialogues portray people doing the real thing. The characters present intellectual and often abstract arguments, that are rebuffed, for sure. And they can be sifted on that level. But we see them running the gamut of human emotion too, for lives lived is ultimately what is at stake.

Seneca wrote the following to a friend:

> The living word and life in common will benefit you more than written discourse. It is to current reality that you must go, first because men believe their eyes more than their ears, and then because the path of precepts is long, but that of examples is short and infallible.

Seneca's is a Platonic sentiment: experience is infallible because it so ably displays human fallibility.

PHILOSOPHY SCHOOL

The dialogues are the most substantial evidence we have that Plato thought Socrates presented philosophy as a way of life. However, it was not only in writing that Plato himself responded to his encounter with Socrates. The seeds of philosophy, as Plato puts it in the *Phaedrus*, find soil to sink roots, time to grow branches, air to spread leaves and the human warmth necessary to produce fruit - fruit that will last - when nurtured with others. Socrates pursued his philosophy with others on the streets of Athens. A generation on, perhaps inevitably as the 'Socratic movement' spread, Plato decided to set up an institution. He acquired an old gymnasium and on the site founded his Academy.

Plato knew that an agnostic approach to philosophy did not just necessitate the ability to form intellectual arguments. As importantly, it needed to be manifest in a way of life. The Academy was designed to develop such a philosophical way of life and train people in it. There was no fee, though a private income that brought the blessing of copious leisure was necessary for any serious attendance. 'Students', if that is the right word, probably wore a simple cloak. Many of them subsequently became statesmen, suggesting something of the atmosphere of the place (though of itself that is not so surprising given the aristocratic nature of much ancient philosophy which meant that many philosophers would naturally go on to rule). Others became famous philosophers in their own right, including Aristotle who attended the school for 20 years. One of Aristotle's pupils, Dicearchus, described the Academy as a

Illus. 6.1:   Plato's Academy aimed at personal transformation as well as
careful understanding.

community in which people were free and equal, and inspired by virtue and research. Many of these values are embodied in the *Republic*, Plato's plan for a perfect city. For example, women could govern as well as men.

Setting up the Academy carried certain risks with it. The idea of a philosophical school might suggest that philosophy was a subject to be taught, that it consisted of a set of doctrines or, worse, necessitated passing examinations: the Academy might become academic. Socrates was peripatetic for these reasons. He did not want to inform - as an agnostic how could he? He wanted to form.

Plato seems to have avoided these pitfalls for the most part, though he clearly moves on from Socrates. For example, one might ask why, alongside the question of how to live, he established disciplines such as geometry, logic and natural science? Might this not be evidence that he started to value abstract thought for its own sake? Not quite. The goal of pursuing what we would call scientific knowledge is not that it represents the last word on truth: Plato calls such an idea ridiculous in the *Republic*. Nor, particularly, that it might find application. Rather, knowledge of nature is most valuable insofar as it makes connections that then become a platform from which more profound insights on the nature of things might be glimpsed. Science is a prelude to philosophy, though a good, even necessary, one. If the *Seventh Letter* is by Plato he explains in his own words why this is the case:

> For this knowledge is not something that can be put into works like other sciences; but after long continued intercourse between teacher and pupil, in joint pursuit of the subject, suddenly, like light flashing forth when a fire is kindled, it is born in the soul and straightway nourishes itself.

The goal of studying science was as a form of exercise to ready the mind for intuitions about the way things are, as opposed to what they are made of - the lesser question that science of itself attempts by direct observation. Plato probably followed the not unreasonable belief of the Pythagoreans who sought to understand the order and harmony of the cosmos as a matter of spirit as well as maths. Or perhaps the sentiment is not unlike Darwin's famous last sentence in *On The Origin of Species*.

There is grandeur in this view of life, with its several powers, having been originally breathed into a few forms or into one; and that,
whilst this planet has gone cycling on according to the fixed law of
gravity, from so simple a beginning endless forms most beautiful
and most wonderful have been, and are being, evolved.

This is more than just a purple passage. The agnostic Darwin, after
developing as many of the details of his revolutionary thesis as he is able,
is reduced to contemplating grandeur - beautiful and wonderful. He is
often remembered for being troubled by the implications of evolution
for his faith. But that should not preclude the sense in which it dis-
closes, not dissolves, a new dimension to the mystery of life.

That this is the spirit within which Plato sought truth might be
thought to be undermined by the fact that his philosophy can and has
been taken as dogmatic. However, what is overlooked here is that any theories he proposed himself, such as that of the Forms, were always hedged
with heavy irony. It is as if he is saying, 'Good idea, but one cannot be sure:
at best they point us beyond.' Again, for him, it is a rationally fired agnosticism that leads to insight, not any crude rational dogmatism. That the
ideas which circulated within the Academy were not treated dogmatically
is also supported by Aristotle's profound disagreement with Plato on
proposals like the Forms, a stance that was shared by the two individuals
who immediately succeeded Plato as head too: there was plenty of room
for disagreement since everything was up for grabs. And it was not until
long after his death that anyone talked of Platonism. In fact, the period of
the Academy's existence from about 250 to 150 BCE, the so-called Middle
Academy, was known particularly for its scepticism, though after that a
more dogmatic Platonism does seem to have taken hold.

SOCRATIC EXERCISES

Spoken dialogue played a central part in the life of the Academy, not
least because being skilled at rhetoric was advantageous to any citizen of

the ancient city-state. However, Plato was wary of oratory for its own sake. In arrogant hands, he thought, it could breed a relativism of the wrong kind, the relativism which acts as if one argument is as good as any other. The best use of dialogue was as an exercise aimed at the transformation of the interlocutors. As Pierre Hadot, the contemporary philosopher who has spearheaded the rediscovery of ancient philosophy as a way of life, explains: 'It was not a matter of combat between two individuals, in which the more skillful person imposed his point of view, but a joint effort on the part of two interlocutors in accord with the rational demands of reasonable discourse.' In other words, the value of expressing yourself clearly was only so as to be able to 'offer' it to another, who had a similarly well-honed argument that, by understanding, you could grasp at a profound level too. The point of so inhabiting another view was to identify with something beyond yourself to take you out of yourself. A partial parallel today would be the seminar in which students have to play the role of opponents in a debate. Another is to think of Platonic dialogue as role playing: Plato calls them 'entertainments' in one place, meaning 'serious play acting'.

Hadot argues that it is right to talk of spiritual exercises in the Academy since this underlines the centrality of experiencing concepts when discussing them, again in line with the goal of a philosophy that is more than rational expression. The idea is that working at this intuitive level — enunciating why such and such does not feel right - was as valid as highlighting logical inconsistencies and flaws. To the same end, students practised other exercises alongside dialogue. One was sexual abstinence (as in Platonic relationships) though it would be a mistake to take that as meaning a negation of passion: the aim this time was to sublimate erotic love and focus its energy and insight on higher things. Another possible exercise had to do with sleep. There is a passage in the *Republic* in which Plato sounds almost Freudian: the 'terrible and savage' dreams he writes about could provide someone with material for reflection. As Chaucer wrote in *The Monk's Tale*, recalling the Delphic inscription: 'Full wise is he that can himself know.'

Another central exercise was the contemplation of death. Death is of interest because it is the moment when one's life's work comes to an end: the person you have become then will be the person you are in eternity. What someone felt about their death revealed much about their attitude to life and how far they had advanced on the way of life of the philosopher.

In Plato's dialogue the *Gorgias*, Socrates tells a myth about the last judgement that captures the right attitude someone should have to their death (similar stories end the *Phaedo* and the *Republic* too, suggesting the importance of this exercise). It used to be the case in primordial times, the myth goes, that people were judged before they died, and by living judges to boot. Depending on how they had lived their lives they would either go to the Isles of the Blessed or to the prison of Tartarus. Now, some cases were being decided badly, an issue that was brought to Zeus' attention by Pluto. Zeus, in his wisdom, noticed that the judges were being misled by the way people dressed up for their judgement - donning their finery in order to look fine in soul too. So, Zeus decreed, people would no longer be told when they are to die and they would be judged on that final day naked. With that change, even when the Great King comes before the throne of judgement he will be judged in the same way as the most humble serf: according to the beauty and perfection, or the distortion and ugliness, of his soul. Socrates tells Callicles, his main interlocutor in the *Gorgias*, that he passionately believes this myth and has taken it to heart:

> I think about how I'll reveal to the judge a soul that's as healthy as it can be. So I disregard the things held in honour by the majority of people, and by practising truth I really try, to the best of my ability, to be and to live as a very good man, and when I die, to die like that.

He calls Callicles to this way of life, because he regards it as worth more than any other. 'Maybe you think this account is told as an old wives' tale, and you feel contempt for it,' he asks. But the point is a right one nonetheless. Philosophical success in life is not about having the right arguments, seeming good or even having acted on conscience. It is about being transformed into someone who is good that a philosopher should care about. The best judge will see a life naked and in its entirety. The many pictures of Socrates serenely drinking the hemlock, that artists have produced down the centuries, can be thought of as reaching back to

this aspect of life in the Academy. The iconography represents the culmination of its way of life as well as a celebration of Socrates.

Silence may have featured in the academician's portfolio too. Silence
was probably a state to which the Pythagoreans aspired - contemplation
of the 'music of the spheres' propelling the individual towards a 'harmonious silence'. And Socrates is depicted in silence at various points in the
dialogues, if often rather oddly and abruptly. He is reported to have once
suddenly stood still, without speaking, for so long that crowds formed
around him. More theologically, he explains, in the *Phaedo*, that the
philosopher's aim is the contemplation of divine things that are beyond
opinion, which is to say beyond the grasp of human words. As he is dying
he commends his followers to silence, since it is in silence that someone
has the best chance of discovering the things that are of heaven.

One question that comes to mind is the extent to which Plato's philosophy school was like a religious institution such as a monastery. The
comparison is only good in part. Although Plato dedicated a statue of
the Muses in the grove that formed part of the site, and his successors
added other devotional objects, the Academy did not exist to worship
any gods or perpetuate a cult; it aimed at the transformation of the individual and the development of a philosophical life. Having said that, as
a disciplined form of life, a monastery and the Academy were perhaps
similar. For one thing, given that the school was full of disagreements
that might easily have led to permanent factions and splits, there must
have been a very powerful sense of common commitment to its ideals to
hold people together. To attend the Academy was to be in love with its
way of life, in the manner of Socrates who was in love with wisdom: students were fulfilling a vocation. More prosaically, it is perhaps not too
fanciful to imagine an unwritten rule of life too, not unlike that of Saint
Benedict, which detailed those things necessary for a communal, pur-
poseful life, like the partitioning of the day. Like Benedictines, members
of the Academy were not averse to feasting either - if in moderation.

THE DIVERSIFICATION OF STYLES

Plato's philosophy school was hugely successful. It carried his own
encounter with Socrates to those who never knew Socrates in person,
not by promoting a set of intellectual principles but by inculcating a

practice. This was shaped by exercises and disciplined by reason but ultimately the goal was to form individuals who saw the world with a philosopher's eyes - preserving the charism of Socrates.

It was a pattern others sort to emulate. After Aristotle left the Academy he formed his own, the Lyceum. From what remains of Aristotle's writings one can infer that he thought the ideal for the good life was to be self-sufficient. His model of the wise individual was someone who had developed the greatest ability to contemplate, an activity of pure attention which the most excellent would engage in alone: 'He has slow movements, a deep voice and calm speech,' Aristotle amusingly writes. Contemplation was key because, at best, it was non-discursive. To speak philosophically is merely to link words together. Meaning comes from within. In practice, this is something that people can only achieve after much training and effort: the school provided the place where things could be explored and discussed in order to train the attention.

After Plato and Aristotle, there are generally reckoned to be four other schools: the Cynics, the Pyrrhonians, the Stoics and the Epicureans. Although they evolved and emphasised different aspects of their ethos over the hundreds of years for which they existed, one can see them all as attempts to form ways of life that face up to the central Socratic insight that nothing of importance in life can be known with certainty and that a way of life is key to embracing the intuitions that come with that agnosticism.

Those that wore the badge of the Cynic were the most extreme. Their approach was to reject even those things that people might regard as minimally necessary in life, such as the need to be clean or the need to be courteous. One might say that cynicism was the radical refusal of all certainties, no matter what, because they were all considered delusional - things like cleanliness and courteousness being mere conventions. The Cynics disturbed many people and are infamous for doing everything from masturbating in public to being rude to kings.

Pyrrhonian suspicion of what people think of as necessary in life manifested itself in a different way. Rather than rejection, this school cultivated indifference. Pyrrho, the individual the founders cited as their inspiration, sought to doubt anything that was not immediately and obviously the case in any particular situation - something that is far harder than it might first seem. He believed that to hold to views, opinions or beliefs - which is what one does when one tries to articulate principles, no matter how vague or general - is a recipe for unhappiness: they are bound to prove uncertain.

Stoic uncertainty manifests itself in a different way again. In short, Stoics thought that life becomes tragic because people struggle to shape things that are external to them and over which they have no control and little understanding. To be stoical is, therefore, to actively embrace one's fate. This does not mean one cannot be morally good: moral goodness is doing what is right in line with fate. The role of reason within Stoicism is to work on a rule of life that is harmonious within itself and with the world as it comes to one.

Finally, the Epicureans. The insight they had about uncertainty is that it leads to fear. However, since uncertainty cannot be done away with, the key is to dissipate the fear. Epicurus argued that people are free to face anything that leads to uncertainty in life without fear - the likelihood of bad health, the unavoidability of death, the capriciousness of the gods. Epicurean philosophy is, therefore, less deterministic than Stoicism: one is free to find as much pleasure in bread and water as a feast, Epicurus said. It is also, in a sense, against reason: Epicurus thought that reason tends to encourage grandiose ideas that, because they can never quite rid themselves of uncertainties, causes 'turmoil in the souls of men'. For this reason, Epicureans liked to say that they were not followers of Socrates, though they would never have existed without him.

CHRISTIAN INNOVATIONS

The philosophical schools, and the ways of life they encouraged, lasted well into the Christian period. Plato's Academy was finally closed by the Emperor Justinian in 529 CE. Their influence on early Christianity is pronounced too. The so-called Desert Fathers of the first centuries after Christ explicitly discussed ancient philosophy and adopted similar practices of asceticism, contemplation and withdrawal from the city - if purified, as they saw it, from the errors of paganism. There are even letters that purport to have been written between Seneca, a great Stoic, and St Paul, in which they offer one another their mutual admiration.

They are completely fanciful but that they were fabricated at all underlines how early Christianity adopted and adapted the Socratic insight in their search for their great unknown, God.

In some ways early Christian practices and the way of life of the ancient philosophers are forms of a not dissimilar spirituality. First, in being uncertain of themselves - the Socratic because they realise they do not know themselves, the Christian because they are born into self-deceiving sin - both are given intimations of what might be called the divine truth that lies beyond them and to which they strive. Second, the exercises by which they move towards this truth of themselves are a work on themselves: followers of Socrates and early Christians were called to ask questions of themselves with a view to a transformation. And third, this spirituality does not conceive of the individual being given truths, as if it were some kind of gnostic reward. Rather, the process itself is its own fulfilment where it becomes a way of life. To borrow a distinction made by Epicurus: in most labours of life, the reward follows when the task is complete; the tougher the task, the more profound the rewards. But with this way of life, 'the learning and the enjoyment are simultaneous'. 'He who looses his life, gains it', is the biblical, more gnomic summary.

One does not need to learn much more of this philosophical tradition that manifested itself as the cultivation of a way of life before an obvious question springs to mind. How is it that what is usually taken as philosophy today seems so different? Why does it apparently make so little demand upon the modern philosopher's person (beyond the development of rational techniques, thought and intellectual know-how)? Philosophers may try to live ethically, as in having good reasons for what they do. But rarely is philosophy taken as being total in the sense of the ancients - a practice that seeks to shape the individual, heart and mind. No professor today would say to his or her students (even less to his or her funders) it is not my lectures or publications that count, but what I am becoming!

Hadot has asked this question and he puts it down to historical developments that came with the institutionalisation of Christianity. Broadly speaking, it may be summed up in two moves. First, over time Christianity tended to treat philosophy more and more as a servant of theology which was taken as revealed by God. The new religion flexed its muscles and built up a body of doctrines with which to govern itself and manage its institutional boundaries. The burden of philosophy's 'job' came to be to elucidate dogma, sidelining the exploration of uncertainties and apophatic theology; more and more it became the handmaid of dogmatic theology not agnosticism. In the same move, the ancient philosophers' approaches became detached from philosophy and, transformed, re-associated with Christian disciplines whose goal was not so much transformation as salvation. Practice tended to became prohibition. Second, philosophy became an autonomous discipline, a separation of heart and mind that was sealed with the emergence of the modern university. It became what Socrates must have feared, a subject to be taught and examined.

MODERN SOCRATICS

Having said that, the separation of philosophy as a conceptual exercise and as a mode of existence was never absolute. And herein lies hope. Throughout the history of ideas in the Christian West, thinkers have regularly lamented the opposition of philosophy as a private art and as a public discourse - suggesting in the process that the two might move closer together once again. Michel de Montaigne achieved a new synthesis in the sixteenth century. He wrote his *Essays* as a therapy to overcome a crushing melancholia. They are philosophical not because he was trained as a philosopher but because they are an analysis of his life - 'assays' of everything from solitude to sleep: 'I am myself the matter of my book', he wrote, forging the way of life of the intellectual writer. He is called the French Socrates and has also been attributed with the revival of an agnostic Pyrrhonism. He had 'Know thyself!' and 'What do I know?' written on the beams of his study-tower and realised that the philosopher's real test was his character not his conclusions.

> The soul which houses philosophy must by her own sanity make for a sound body. Her tranquility and ease must flow from her; she must fashion her outward bearing to her mould, arming it therefore with gracious pride, a spritely active demeanour and a happy welcoming face. The most express sign of wisdom is unruffled joy: like all the realms above the Moon, her state is ever serene.

156

Illus. 6.2: Michel de Montaigne 'assayed' his life in the privacy of the tower of the Château de Montaigne, Périgord.

A more recent example of a philosopher for whom his living became increasingly integrated with his thought was Michel Foucault. He too noticed the difference between ancient and modern philosophy, describing it in moral terms. The ancient philosophers elaborated their life as a creative exercise of their moral will, he said. With Christianity, though, morality came to be conceived of as obedience to a code or rules. The difference is not that the former was libertarian and the latter authoritarian; both could be tough ways of life. The difference is that one led to the cutivation of a way of life, the other to a submission of one's life.

The reason this distinction was of interest to Foucault stemmed from his belief that it profoundly shapes the way people live today even in the secular world. He saw this ethic of submission in the way people routinely regulate their behaviour and defer to what is thought normal, whether that be expressed in adhering to dress codes for the office or in the way that ethics as a whole is thought of in terms of rules. The difference is well captured in an essay, entitled 'The Good Man', by D. H. Lawrence.

> The *homme de bien*, the good man, performs the robot trick of isolating himself from the great passions. For the passion of life he · substitutes the reasonable social virtues ...
>
> Now the 'good man' is all right as far as he goes. One must be honest in one's dealings, and one does feel kindly towards the poor ... The trouble with the 'good man' is that he's only one-hundredth part of a man.

The problem for Foucault, and for us, is that one cannot simply wind back the clock and reinstate the old philosophy. The modern way of life with its pervasive codes of behaviour does not readily allow it. But as a first step, at least, in his last works, Foucault developed a more modest task for contemporary philosophy. It could begin with the effort to think differently - another way of pushing at uncertainty. Philosophy could study the past not so much to recover what might otherwise be lost, nor to weigh up the ethical dilemmas ancient people faced. Rather, as a new form of philosophical exercise that might suggest new ways of re-imagining the present. At a personal level, for Foucault, one manifestation of this was in relation to his homosexuality. Received wisdom in gay culture is that liberation means coming out. However, by contrasting the modern understanding of gayness that designates a form of human behaviour with ancient attitudes towards same-sex couples where it was seen as an expression of socialisation and love, Foucault argued that the contemporary label of homosexual could be oppressive regardless of whether someone was open about their sexuality or not. This suggested a further philosophical exercise that sought a way beyond the prioritisation of sexuality as a determining characteristic of the individual - a 'way out' of sexuality as he put it.

NOT SO ACADEMIC

Montaigne and Foucault stand out as two examples of philosophers who explicitly engaged with Socrates in his agnosticism and Plato in his emphasis on a way of life. However, the connection between principle and practice seems to force its way, as it were, into the lives of other philosophers who might otherwise be thought purely academic.

Consider Descartes, the man who doubted everything until he was left only with the thinking 'I'. It might be thought that nothing could be more removed from life than that. And yet, he derived his famous 'Je pense, donc je suis' in the context of a meditation. It leads the reader through feelings as well as thoughts. The aim seems to be twofold. First, the meditations were not supposed to inculcate radical doubt for its own sake but to reveal to the philosopher the limits of human reason. Second, Descartes believed that someone needs to be in the right position to receive truth, as well as to have the right arguments. Meditation could lead to the construction of such an attitude. Hume made not dissimilar suggestions. He discussed a kind of passive cognition that happens to us. One must make preparations to be open to it, preparations that would connect the philosophy to the life.

Or take a philosopher like Schopenhauer. He is famous for his pessimism and explicitly said that philosophy cannot change lives. He thought human beings were the tragic slaves of their base wills. People may make great efforts to aspire to the higher things that their 'excess intellect' glimpses above them; but will 'will out'. Love, for example, is always brutalised by the animal will for coitus. The result, some of his interpreters say, is suffering and labour and radical unhappiness. This though is not quite fair. Every day Schopenhauer read from the *Upanishads*. They confirmed for him a rather different ethic: if the world is determined by will, then the goal of life should be to overcome that endless volition. He interpreted nirvana as the end of wilfulness which because it is never fully possible in this life would be like a transition to nothingness. In other words, philosophy for Schopenhauer was like the Eastern teaching that the value of life lies in not wanting it - and that required the cultivation of an attitude to life, not just thought about it. Even for Schopenhauer, and almost in spite of himself, philosophy elicits a way of life.

Conversely, consider Karl Popper. The writer Bryan Magee, who often visited Popper in his hermit-like cottage, says that he was not an easy man to know. However, Magee explains: 'A phrase I heard from his lips as often as any other was, "We don't know anything." He looked on this realisation, which he attributed historically to Socrates, as the most important philosophical insight there is, one which ought to inform all our philosophical activity.' For Popper, certainty is not available to human beings because all human knowledge is capable of being revised. What is taken as knowledge at any particular time must, therefore, be only an approximation to the truth. This is the basis of his most well-known theoretic contribution - the theory of falsification in science. However, what can be overlooked is the impact this thesis had upon his life. In his intellectual autobiography, significantly entitled *Unended Quest*, he repeatedly testifies to his contentment. He goes so far as to say that he knows of no happier philosopher. The source of his happiness is intimately connected to the unknowability of the world. At a mundane level, this unknowability means that one is constantly surprised by what one finds in the world around one: 'One of the many great sources of happiness is to get a glimpse, here and there, of a new aspect of the incredible world we live in, and of our incredible role in it,' he writes. More philosophically, he says that it is in his engagement with problems, theories and arguments - the abstractions that people wrestle with as they learn more profoundly about what they do not know - that he has found more happiness than he could ever deserve.

Reclaiming the Religious

In the last chapter, I tried to give an account of a Christian agnosticism as one response to the potency found in the essential unknowability of life. In this chapter, we have picked up on the tradition in philosophy that leads back to Plato and Socrates. So now, a good question to ask is whether, and if so how, these two elements might come together?

It might be tempting to sift some flattering virtues that would be thought distinctive of such an attitude, to draw out similarities and differences between them and, say, the Christian who aspires to love and forgiveness or the humanist who lauds tolerance and justice. The agnostic ethos might be thought to value courage and integrity in its engagement with the unknown. However, there is something misleading in this approach. For one thing, these virtues are far from exclusive to the agnostic. And they also put the cart before the horse. Virtues arise from an ethos not out of the ether.

But there is a word that captures the agnostic way of seeing for which I am arguing. It is a word that we have already explored at some length, namely, the word religious. There is, of course, a risk in using this word. To many to be religious is to be the opposite of agnostic (when the word agnostic is taken to signify 'a man without qualities', in Robert Musil's phrase). However, I want to reclaim them both, for to be properly agnostic is, I believe, to be religious - religious in the sense that I used it at the start: the sense and taste for the Infinite, the search for intuitions of being-itself.

Why a religious agnosticism? In a word, Socrates. For him, a sense of the unknown divine was essential for framing his understanding of the human lot. He was a philosopher because he understood human beings are between beasts and angels. He was a philosopher because he dared to contemplate his ignorance. A powerful religious sensibility was part and parcel of this way of life. Socrates was interested in theology - god-talk - not because he thought it would tell him much about deities but because he thought it threw human beings onto a consciousness of their limits. When discussing whether things are good because a god says so, or whether the god says they are good because they are good in themselves, the direction the inquiry takes him is not to question whether

the gods are necessary to morality but to show how little humans un̲
stand about moral good.

Socrates was a sceptic of the humble sort. He accepted that just because he could not understand something, that did not mean there was not wisdom to be had in ancient traditions, and religious traditions in particular. At their best they, like him, were engaged in the big questions of life. After all, it was an oracle, an utterer of mysteries, that kick-started his philosophical life. Socrates' religiousness also comes across as an expression of the way his philosophy engaged him heart and mind. His rational brilliance was accompanied by an inner daemon that expressed inarticulate uncertainties to him. He was called a philosopher because of his great love, not because of any wisdom he possessed. He was religious because it was wonder that drove him, and led him to toy at the most profound levels of his being with the religious injunction, 'Know thyself!'.

With Socrates, we saw how the religious milieu of Ancient Athens provided him with an immediate context, as it were, to develop his agnostic way of life. The question is whether the religious and scientific milieu that we find ourselves in today can provide some similar basis from which to develop a contemporary equivalent. Apart from the further reflections in this chapter, this is what I have attempted to do in the chapters on science and on religion. With science I argued that an agnostic will be led to an attitude of appreciative and critical wonderment - the sense that, at the limits of a scientific understanding, the human imagination is thrown onto other ways of seeking meaning, value and knowledge. With religion there is some more to add now.

John Caputo has written a short book which is very helpful in this respect, called *On Religion*. In it he argues that, on the one hand, many people who might think of themselves as religious because they go to church are, in fact, not, because what they seek from church is certainty. Then, on the other hand, there are those who would never darken the doors of a church but are actually profoundly religious, because they actively embrace the uncertainties of life. For Caputo what makes someone religious, as opposed to religiose, is summed up in two quintessentially religious moments celebrated in the Christian tradition.

The first is when Mary says to the angel, 'Be it unto me according to thy word'. Her pregnancy is an apparent impossibility, but she says 'yes' nonetheless. The power of the story, Caputo says (incidentally, following Derrida's idea of religion without religion), is in the way it conveys that to be religious is to affirm what is on the edge of experience.

The second religious moment is found in Augustine when he asks what does he love when he loves God. This characterises that part of the religious spirit which is uncertain about what it seeks, because it is unknown, but that still seeks it with a passion. It would not be hard to make a comparison with Socrates, the lover of much pursued wisdom.

Having drawn the distinction, Caputo recognises that the religious owe the religiose a debt, for if the former major on the charism, the latter are often the one's who preserve the Church - the traditions upon which both draw. Slightly shifting the distinction, I have come to think of the relationship between a religious sensibility and the institutional Church as two lines moving up a page - representing the passage of time. Sometimes the lines move closely and in parallel. Sometimes they veer wildly apart. When I was a priest and rows flared in the parish about the placing of candlesticks or the wearing of cassocks (oh yes - and I was involved in both), the lines were well apart. At an institutional level, the same could be said of churches in their bureaucratic and officious guises.

Socrates, in a sense, had the advantage of being able to draw directly on the religious milieu of his age in order to inform his philosophical practice (though it proved too much for the authorities in the end). Today, the agnostic must sift the religious practice of believers and the religious discourse of dogmatic theology in search of the apophatic. However, the effort is invaluable, for one is rewarded with a rich resource for contemplating the indissoluble, endlessly perplexing issues that lie behind the big questions which fire the human and, I would argue, philosophical imagination - those that revolve around the 'why' of existence.

It is the religious imagination that I would argue mostly successfully brings together the elements necessary for an agnostic ethos: rational rigour - exemplified by Thomas and the mystical theologians; intellectual commonsense - for the wisdom that alerts one to the wilder fantasies of scientism; heart and mind - for a philosophy that can become a way of life. For me, now, the importance of the religious imagination is that it broadens out what could otherwise be a purely sceptical intellectualism. It adds flesh to the bones, and suggests far more than just an argument. It is manifest in the attitude that sees new discoveries and theories as expressions of what is still not known, rather than as some kind of human triumph. It is manifest in the attitude that sees the goal of the intellectual life as a falling into silence - a contemplation full of texture and colour that is born of the struggle to appreciate the extent of the unknown, which may be called God.

Plato's response to Socrates was to set up a philosophy school. It turned principles into practices, to cultivate a way of life that looked beyond what could be simply rationally settled. Some of those exercises are perfectly doable today. There is no reason why academic philosophy should not be a way to experience thought as well has have it. The right course could even provide space for the contemplation of death! Similarly, silence is to be found in some churches and retreats - and I suspect it is actually not that rare to find yourself sitting next to a wondering scientist. But does the spirit of the old exercises allow for an update and diversification of their forms too? Can Socratic agnosticism be practised throughout modern life? Can it become a way of seeing the world and shaping existence in ways beyond the strictly philosophical or religious? The aphoristic A-Z of the last chapter offers a few suggestions as to how.

How to Be an Agnostic: an Aphoristic A-Z

The darkest place is always underneath the lamp.

Chinese proverb

HEGEL ONCE REMARKED: 'The owl of Minerva spreads its wings only with the falling of the dusk.' Mary Midgley deploys the image in her memoir: 'The thought for which I want to use it is that wisdom, and therefore philosophy, comes into its own when things become dark and difficult rather than when they are clear and straightforward. That - it seems to me - is why it is so important.'

She laments what might be called the gnostic conception of philosophy by telling the story of a man looking for a lost key. Someone walked by and noticed that he was looking only under the lamp-post. 'Is that where it was mislaid?', they ask. 'No', he replies. 'But it is the easy place to look.'

The metaphor and the story could stand for the difference between the life of uncertainty and certainty. What does it look like in practice? How can one be an agnostic? Some suggestions, long and short, in the form of an aphoristic A-Z.

A - is for Agnosticism

'I have observed that the world has suffered far less from ignorance than from pretensions to knowledge. It is not skeptics or explorers but fanatics and ideologues who menace decency and progress. No agnostic ever burned anyone at the stake or tortured a pagan, a heretic, or an unbeliever.' Daniel J. Boorstin.

B - REMEMBERS FRANCIS BACON

On confusing the study of science with the study of things human, moral and divine, Bacon wrote: 'They do not wisely mingle or confound these learnings together.'

C - IS FOR CHURCH

When I was ordained, my bishop, David Jenkins, said that the trouble with the Church is that you can't live with it and you can't live without it. I live without it more than I did. However, for all the criticisms I have made of it, particularly its joining in the battle for certainties, it holds traditions that in my view our world is infinitely poorer without. Where else in our culture can you be ashed, held, and told you are dust and going to die? Where else can you hear otherworldly music enacted in an equally otherworldly context, namely, ancient liturgy? Where else can you sit next to strangers and have remembered before you a story that strains for the divine (though that is often ruined with the 'self-help' Jesus)? Sometimes it is a relief to have the burden of being oneself lifted! Love it and hate it, Church is the place for that.

D - IS ABOUT DARWINISM

Neo-Darwinism is currently the most strident form of scientism. But need one feel in league with the creationists to question it? No. As a starting point, consider the philosophical interpretation of Darwinism offered by Karl Popper. For him, Darwinism is not a testable scientific theory but what he called a 'metaphysical research programme' within which many theories might be tested. One should not get carried away with this metaphysical ascription. He did not mean it in any theological sense, but simply to suggest that Darwinism as a whole is not falsifiable and so not of the best kind of theory science can offer.

In fact, in a certain way, Darwinian adaption is tautologous. If you imagine a fairly stable environment in which a species of fairly similar reproducing creatures live, then the offspring of those creatures that are better adapted to that environment are bound to survive more readily.

What Darwinism adds to this picture - and the thing that Popper thought of as its greatest scientific achievement - is that the evolution of species will be gradual; it will occur over long periods of time (though rates of evolutionary change are typically far from clear).

There are two striking things over which Darwinism struggles. The first is the origin of life. It is possible that at some point in the future scientists who mimic what they take to be a primordial soup in the laboratory will show that certain complex molecules can take on some of the properties necessary for life, such as replication. However, it is vastly improbable that anything that could be called life would emerge from such experiments, and that is according to Darwinism: our planet required enormously long periods of time for life to emerge.

The second is the variety of life. This might be thought surprising. After all, is it not obvious when reproduction and small variations between the generations are coupled to natural selection that an abundance of life is the inevitable result, given time? Popper refutes this with a thought experiment. Say life was discovered on Mars, but only in the form of one type of primitive bacterium. Would people say that Darwinism had been refuted? No: they would say that only one bacterium was well enough adapted to survive. So Darwinism does not pre dict the variety of the species we see on earth. Neither does it offer a particularly satisfactory mechanism to explain it. In fact, how separate species evolve, as opposed to the variations within species, is one of the hottest subjects for study, and speculation, in biology. What is not clear is how natural selection might lead to the discontinuities between species - the moment when gene transmission stops - if species themselves are the result of transmitted changes in organisms.

Where Darwinism is at its strongest is in relation to adaption within species. One of its greatest benefits is in relation to disease: understanding how bacteria and viruses mutate is of enormous use in the development of drug therapies. Popper also thought that Darwinism is an excellent basis upon which to devise certain research programmes: studying why and how organisms adapt is one obvious possibility, manifest particularly in modern genetics.

However, beyond these substantial areas of research, Darwinism as a science moves onto thinner ice. Take, for example, the question of why what might be called higher functions of living animals evolved - like consciousness. Evolutionary psychologists will say that consciousness evolved because it is adaptive; it has causal efficacy in the survival of the species concerned. But that is to say no more than that consciousness exists, albeit in Darwinian terms. What it does not do is capture the experience of consciousness itself. What it is to experience oneself as a subject is simply beyond science. (I think the evidence is that it is beyond philosophy to explain consciousness too without invoking the idea that there are two kinds of substances in the world - physical ones like brain-states, and mental ones like experiences.)

Where Darwinian thought is not just inadequate but completely falls apart, in my opinion, is in relation to theories such as memes. According to its advocates, memes are the mental equivalent of genes. Anything that can be thought and is replicated - from a philosophical argument to a cultural icon - would be a meme. What memes are supposed to explain is the transmission of ideas: they compete and only the fittest survive. The advocates of memes usually ascribe religious memes the honour of being the most pernicious, saying that the religious imperative to replicate - to proselytise - reveals its selfish intent.

Why are memes such a bad theory? For one thing, it has a woefully impoverished understanding of the entities that memes are supposed to pass on. It is not in the nature of all religions to proselytise, for example. (It is only Christianity that has done so throughout its history with any vigour.) Neither does meme theory have much conception of the environment in which they are supposed to interact. Ideas, for example, spread as a result of the way they interact with people, times and places: one must understand those people, times and places in order to understand why ideas spread. Finally, memes fall foul of a category error. Genetic evolution works relatively well as a way of understanding biological species, but to take that theory and apply it to cultural and social phenomena is as mistaken as thinking that gravity is the reason people are attracted to one another.

So where does this leave the agnostic in relation to Darwinian science? First, in emphasising its limits one can appreciate its successes. Darwin's brilliant idea explains much: from why superbugs resist penicillin to why life takes eons to evolve. However, it does not explain

'99 per cent of life', as some of its advocates declare. There is far more for biology to do than simply a little tidying up.

Darwin will be superseded, as surely as Newton was by Einstein. This is not to say evolution is wrong; only that it is no more or less than the best theory we have to date. Given that, its limits are causes for wonderment. Darwinism draws our attention to the unaccountable plethora of species. Its partial suggestions as to why there are so many, emphasises all the more the astonishing prodigiousness of life.

E - IS FOR ETHOS

Melvyn Bragg was interviewed on the BBC's radio programme *Devout Sceptics*. He was asked in what sense he was an agnostic. He said: 'One of the greatest phrases I heard in the last two or three years was Issac Newton's answer to someone who asked him how he discovered the laws of gravity, which changed life profoundly, and he said, "By thinking on it continually." And I keep thinking about that phrase and think that if I keep thinking on things continually ... you never know what will happen.'

F - IS ABOUT FACTS

In his essay, 'The Decay of Lying', Oscar Wilde decries what he calls the 'monstrous worship of facts': 'There is something truly monstrous about scientific curiosity because it seems to extend to facts something they do not deserve. Facts must be respected but never worshipped.'

G - IS ON GOD

[silence]

H - IS FOR HISTORY

Today's appetite for history is striking. In many bookshops the history section is second in size only to fiction. On TV, history programmes command very respectable audience figures, that rise even more if they

build in an element of celebrity. History as heritage is a similarly growing industry. So why is history so popular?

It must be partly because history is communicated so well. As Simon
Schama has argued in his book, notably entitled, *Dead Certainties*, 'the
asking of questions and the relating of narratives need not ... be mutually
exclusive forms of historical representation'. In other words, it is perfectly respectable to treat history as 'a work of the imagination'. Long
gone are the days when it was merely learning dates by rote.

However, underneath this excellent synthesis of style and substance,
lies a human need that reaches back to Socrates: the need to know who
we are and where we have come from. I have not done any empirical
research, but I would not be surprised if the rise of history coincides
with the decline of religion. Perhaps religion remains strong in the US
because history has far fewer seams to mine and the country understands itself more of as an idea than a tradition.

In other words, history fulfills some of the functions performed by
religion. At one level, it provides a narrative within which people can
situate themselves: the way history is recalled, researched and related is
as much a story of the present as of the past. History also tends to be the
story of men and women of consequence, and thus a flattering and fascinating mode of inquiry for those majority of us who are not. But where
history's religious shape is seen most clearly is in the way it takes one
out of oneself. It achieves this sense of personal perspective by retelling
events that are simultaneously familiar and distant. The familiar aspects
allow us to empathise with the past, to see ourselves in it. The distant
aspects stem from the radical differences of experience and existence
that separate times and places. The combination of the two aspects
means that we become strangers to ourselves in the process of learning
about it.

The romantic poets were articulate advocates of this religious view of
history. Take two poems of John Keats. In 'Ode to a Nightingale', the
'full-throated ease' of the bird's song provides an intimation of immortality to the death-dreading young man. But the creature, that was 'not
born for death', provides a bridge between the present and the otherwise unbridgeable past. 'The voice I hear this passing night was heard /
In ancient days by emperor and clown.' Its song is a form of ecstasy

because it takes Keats out of himself in this way. Indeed, it is not just long-dead persons with whom he thereby senses his connection and disconnection. The nightingale enables him to empathise with the biblical character of Ruth and fictional 'sprites' too.

History as a meditation on mortality is the central theme of another of Keats's poems, 'Ode on a Grecian Urn'. Much of the poem describes the deities and mortals, the maidens and satyrs, the priest and lovers pictured on the urn. Keats notices how these figures stand outside of time and how blessed that frozen state is. The lovers who almost kiss will love each other forever because they will always be winning their goal. The trees will never be bare. The pipers never short of song. In the beauty of the urn and the portrayal of this timelessness Keats can equate beauty with truth, truth with beauty. Its eternal history transports him from his own temporality: 'Thou, silent form, dost tease us out of thought / As doth eternity'.

History on the TV and in books is clearly not always so intensely felt as the romantics would have it. But in its tales of tragedy and triumph, of humdrum and high-powered lives, it conjures up the same ambivalent feelings of familiarity and distance. Inasmuch as it exists on the borders of what is known and unknown, history is an excellent provocation of the mystery of things.

I - IS FOR IMAGINATION

'At the moment of performance you immerse yourself so much in the music that it becomes a kind of palliative or ersatz religion.' John Elliot Gardner.

K - IS FOR KANT

Immanuel Kant argued that all scientific and moral judgements are imposed by the mind on the world; that is the only way we can apprehend things. Not that things dó not exist. It is just that we cannot know what they are as things in themselves. So there is the world of phenomena, the apparent world, and the world of noumena - the unknown 'thing in itself'. Kant called this transcendental idealism, meaning that the noumenal world can be inferred from reason but is itself another order of being. By subtle and circuitous routes in his *Critiques* he sought to describe exactly what can be said by reason and what cannot. Ultimately, he saw the identification of the noumenal world as evidence for the existence of God - because it is unknown.

L - IS FOR LOVE

In the *Symposium*, Plato records two myths that tell of the origins of love. They present diametrically opposed conceptions of desire.

The first is put into the mouth of Aristophanes. At first, he says, people were whole. They looked like wheels - rounded and complete. But, being mortals, they were hugely ambitious. They planned an attempt on the gods, an invasion of heaven. Needless to say, they did not succeed and Zeus punished them by cutting them in two, so that they would lose their strength. As he cut them, Apollo turned their heads around so that they could see the wound.

Next though, looking at what he had done, Zeus took pity upon the lost, dismembered halflings. So, he moved their genitals around too, placing them beneath their heads, in order to provide a way for them to reconnect with their lost halves and see the joy in the other half's face as it happened. This is the origin of love: to find the lost half of our original whole, to make one out of two, and heal the pain of loneliness and alienation. The power of love is nothing less than the desire to be made complete. The ecstasy of love-making is the annihilation of the separate self in the other.

This myth captures the irresistible nature of love very well. It conveys the extraordinary lengths people will go to for love, the blindness that lovers have to their own faults and the world around them, and the agony that they go through should they be separated once more.

However, it also perpetuates the idea that love can be completed. It feeds into the romantic myth that there is someone out there for you, who, once found, will perfect your life. What can be overlooked is its dark undercurrents. Should two people find their lost halves in each other, the myth says that their embrace is total. Aristophanes imagines Hephaestus passing by two such lovers and asking them what they want. Being the craftsman god, they ask him to weld them together. Once so fused, the lovers are unable to move. It is as if they are dead.

Socrates relates the second myth which was given to him by Diotima, the priestess. It is the tale of the birth of Eros, following the sexual congress of Penia and Poros, poverty and resourceful cunning. This myth portrays love as a desire for what one lacks too but, unlike Aristophanes' myth, that lack can never be wholly satisfied by finding a lover. Neither does it seek only lovers, for it strives ultimately for wisdom.

Moreover, Eros himself is not a god, but moves in between the realm of the gods and human beings. In other words, that human beings love is simultaneously the sign that they aspire to divine things, though they can never reach them. After all, gods do not love, for they lack nothing. Whatever the joys of such an existence might be, they are not the joys of what human love can achieve, like children (a pregnancy of the body, Diotima says) and philosophy (a pregnancy of the soul).

Socrates' encounter with Diotima does not stop there. She tells him that if the origins of Eros is the lower mystery of love, the higher mystery is the upper path along which love can lead someone. This is the famous ascent of the *Symposium*. What it describes is the way that love's continuous desire for what is true leads the individual from loving others to loving beautiful things, to eventually loving what is beautiful itself. Like the light that leaps from a diamond, hiding the gem itself, this is a theophany, a sense of the divine, a glimpse of something too beautiful to grasp in its entirety. The test is the beautiful things the vision inspires in people's lives - the love the individual shows.

Diotima's ascent inspired a whole tradition within philosophy. In Platonism, the mystery that Diotima described to Socrates becomes an ontology. For example, in Plotinus, the goal of loving is a transcendent unity, and human beings can reach out to it because this One itself gives forth divine emanations. One of the most powerful adaptations of Diotima's mystery is found in Augustine. Many will know of his famous comment that our hearts are restless until they find rest in God. God is, here, being identified with the climax of Diotima's ascent. If one recalls the unknowability of God that is a central theme in Augustine, then part of what he is saying is that love itself is a mystery: like Socrates who never ceased loving, because wisdom always ultimately eluded him,

Augustine remained a lover of God, who was the goal of the pilgrimage of his whole life.

Someone might complain that this presents a perpetually frustrated picture of love. They would prefer Aristophanes' view in which love can come to an end, even if in a form of death. However, the more profound interpretation that Augustine places on love is that to love is to be thrown onto the nature of existence itself. Put more colloquially, it is why lovers say, 'I am glad you are alive': in loving they realise that they are alive themselves. The mystery of love is not to be found in its satisfaction, but simply in the attempt to love - to live ever more fully.

M - IS FOR MOUNTAINS

In 2002, Tate Britain displayed a number of landscape artists, well known in the US though hardly ever seen on the other side of the Atlantic, in an exhibition entitled 'American Sublime'. With their massive mountains, rolling plains, towering clouds and vivid light, these artists of the so-called Hudson River School played with nature and scale in a way that both frightens and inspires. The pictures evoke the sense which, as Edmund Burke wrote, is 'when we have an idea of pain and danger, without being actually in such circumstances. Whatever excites this delight, I call sublime.'

The connection between wonderment and sublime is to do with the overpowering sense that is inspired in such landscape, suggesting that there are values intrinsic in nature that human beings should respect as well as study. This can be forgotten. Scholars suggest that, in its American guise, sublime landscape connects directly with the religious origins of the country. The West, for example, was called God's country. Paintings can suggest that the New World is an emanation of the divine. Holiness and spirituality are then readily coupled to national pride and destiny. Thus, as the professor of art history Roger Hull writes:

> American nature was emblematic of America's size, strength, cultural and economic potential, and materialistic potential. American nature was unlike any other in the world, and certainly different

(and by implication 'better') than the old, used, domesticated nature of England and Europe. William Cullen Bryant urged his friend Thomas Cole, the American landscape painter who had been born in England, to soak up in his imagination 'that wilder image' of American scenery before he took a trip to England and the continent. Bryant's advice was a warning to Cole to remember the virility of American nature and not be seduced by the gentler forms of nature he would encounter on his trip.

This sensibility is therefore very different from that of the agnostic. For people like Bryant, at least, landscape is expressive of what human beings are capable of, not of their limits.

The opposing view is found in the writings of nineteenth-century agnostic and mountaineer, Leslie Stephen. His book *The Playground of Europe*, in which he describes the peaks of the Alps, is still in print. He argued that, before the industrial era, most peoples had just feared mountains. Now, though, in what was called the golden age of mountaineering, they loved them because, though climbable, they challenge. For climbing a mountain is not the same as conquering it (as in the thought that men and women can conquer nature). Rather, mountains return the climber to a place of solitude that modern life has otherwise banished.

The qualities which strike every sensitive observer are impressed upon the mountaineer with tenfold force and intensity. If he is accessible to poetical influences as his neighbours - and I don't know why he should be less so - he has opened new avenues of access between the scenery and his mind. He has learnt a language which is but partially revealed to ordinary men.

Stephen emphasises the importance of experiencing the mountain, not just seeing it from afar, even less reading about it - echoing, perhaps, the Socratic insight that philosophy must be lived and not merely spoken.

I might go on indefinitely recalling the strangely impressive scenes that frequently startle the traveller in the waste upper world; but language is feeble indeed to convey even a glimmering of what is to be seen to those who have not seen it for themselves, whilst to them it can be little more than a peg upon which to hand their own recollections. These glories, in which the mountain Spirit reveals himself to his true worshippers, are only to be gained by the appropriate service of climbing - at some risk, though a very trifling risk, if he is approached with due form and ceremony - into the further recesses of his shrines.

As Anthony Kenny points out in his essay on Stephen in *The Unknown God*, Stephen was at odds with John Ruskin here. Ruskin was another mountain enthusiast but one who thought that the appeal of mountains was like that of cathedrals: they were reflections of superior human sensibilities, not themselves superior to thought. In mountains, Ruskin was reminded of what humanity is capable. Stephen disagreed. In his essay, *An Agnostic's Apology*, his final complaint was against the arrogance of the theist and atheist in the way they ride roughshod over ultimate mystery.

[Agnostics] will be content to admit openly, what you whisper under your breath or hide in technical jargon, that the ancient secret is secret still, that man knows nothing of the Infinite and Absolute; and that, knowing nothing, he had better not be dogmatic about his ignorance.

Mountains evoked in him the same humility: 'Their voice is mystic and has found discordant interpreters: but to me at least it speaks in tones at once more tender and more awe-inspiring than that of any mortal teacher.' His is the agnostic attitude. After all, only faith can move mountains.

N - IS ABOUT NEUROSIS

Freud thought religion infantile. In *The Future of an Illusion*, he argued that it would become clearer and clearer to humanity that religion was an obsessional neurosis which, like children negotiating the reality of their fathers, arises out of the Oedipus complex. 'If this view is right, it is to

Illus. 7.1: Leslie Stephen's agnosticism found expression in his love of the Alps.

be supposed that a turning-away from religion is bound to occur with the fatal inevitability of a process of growth and that we find ourselves at this very juncture in the middle of that phrase of development,' he wrote. It is not clear over what time-scale Freud saw this fatal inevitability emerging but 80 years on there is little sign of the turning-away.

It is commonplace to note that Freud's desire to do away with religion has an Oedipal structure itself: Judaism was the religion of his fathers. Jonathan Lear, in his philosophical introduction *Freud*, makes a more novel observation. He compares Freud's conception of religion with that of Kierkegaard, who thought Christianity, in practice, a monstrous illusion too. However, for Kierkegaard, the ramifications could not have been more different. Kierkegaard interpreted the illusion of religion as a sign that the Christians of his time were not being authentically religious at all. The way they practised their religion was 'a misleading fantasy of religious commitment', as Lear puts it. For Kierkegaard, the future of the illusion was not a turning-away from religion but a struggle with faith proper.

What this suggests about Freud is that he saw religion through the lens of a larger conception of scientific progress, part of which included shaking off the vestiges of what he took to be consolatory beliefs. Reason and experience - what he interestingly called 'our God Logos' - will show that religion is not compatible with the evidence. It is a thought, dare one say an illusion, that has common currency to this day (though, in another twist, the atheists, who follow the same *logos*-god as Freud, now commonly decry Freudianism for its lack of scientific veracity - another Oedipal moment perhaps, if Freud is thought of as one of the fathers of modern atheism).

Today, Christianity seems to operate with an illusion - the illusion of its incompatibility with science. It feels or is forced to compete for the same ground - the ground marked out by the scientific criteria of fact, proof and relevancy. Kierkegaard's call would be to recover a conception of religion that is truer to itself. For him, that call was to radical faith, interpreted as a total lack of reason. Here, I have argued it is to the radical unknowability of God that needs to be recalled, to the extent represented by a passionate agnosticism. Rather than debunking reason, this is an approach that focusses on reason's limits.

O - IS ON OUR PLACE IN THE UNIVERSE

'In between beasts and angels.' Augustine.

P - IS FOR PHILOSOPHY

When I left the Church it was exhilarating. Living waters of enlightenment thought were mine for the imbibing in a new phase of life. So it
surprised me 18 months or so later when I had a minor breakdown.

The presenting symptoms of my collapse were not unusual: a love
affair that did not work out. That I could not stop weeping for days after
its denouement, so much so that I had to hide away in a friend's house,
was a sign that something more substantial was wrong. I had precipi-
tous dreams in which I fell down dark tunnels and woke up conscious of
living in a godless world.

Once my ego managed to gather itself again, I interpreted this flood
of feeling as my emotions catching up with what had been an almost
wholly mental decision to doff the clerical collar. This, I reckoned, must
be what it is like to stare the *nihil* in the face. The question was whether
I had the courage to continue in what I then took to be an ultimately
meaningless life. I envisaged the experience as a kind of rite of passage:
my whole person had now been born into atheism.

Then I lost faith with godlessness because of what seemed to me to be
its poverty of spirit. So now, when I think back on the breakdown it
poses a more general challenge. The emotional trauma was to do with
feeling for sure, and the way that my mind had forced my spirit to run
without the support of the Church before it could walk. But now I
think that it also represented the vital importance of feeling a way into
meaningfulness as well as thinking it, the need to give voice to the
heart's reasons, which reason does not understand.

This, then, is what I take to be the key challenge of belief, at its best,
to the atheist and agnostic alike. It is love's knowledge that counts in
life, not reason (be that in assertive mode or in doubt). This is what
churchgoing, again at its best, nurtures. It is called devotion. When I do
go to church, after atheism, it is this sensibility that I am reminded of.
What might an agnostic's devotion be?

The study of Plato's dialogues was a first step for me. I realised that these texts could be read and re-read because, like religious texts, they simultaneously operate at many levels. The rational is only the level that strikes one first, because academe is inclined to read them in that way. But you cannot miss that these are not treatises. For one thing, Plato presents all sorts of views, arguments and counter-arguments, in the dialogues. Scholars debate and sometimes settle what they regard as Plato's most likely opinion; they draw attention to where his logic falls short. But, valuable though that is, it is only part of the response Plato sought to evoke.

For they are philosophical dramas too. The characters do not merely represent positions but play a part in the debate. In the *Symposium*, immediately after Diotima has described the pinnacle of the ascent and the goal of loving, the Form of Beauty springs into view. But the very next thing that happens is that Alcibiades, a goal of loving and form of beauty as widely celebrated in ancient Athens as David Beckham is today, similarly 'springs' into view as he bursts into the room. The word used for both epiphanies is exactly the same - *exaiphnēs*. Plato is not just questioning his metaphysics, he is mocking it. What can he mean by that?

Alternatively, take a dialogue like the *Phaedo*. Set on the last day of Socrates' life, and culminating in his consumption of the hemlock and final breath, this is a piece of writing that moves seamlessly between thought and feeling. It embraces the quest for meaning at every level, from the reason why Socrates turned from science to philosophy to the high emotion of his death.

In other words, these are texts that one can be devoted to, in a sense very similar to the way people study religious scriptures. This might be a definition of all great literary works. It is why we return to the work of Montaigne, Nietzsche, Shakespeare, Proust, Augustine, Schopenhauer and others.

This is a philosophy that seeks not to win an argument but to cultivate a way of life. By showing as well as telling, Plato managed to convey the Socratic ethos. In the gap between the writing on the page and the life of the reader arise suggestions as to how his questioning quest might be incarnated again. The aim is to engage not only at the intellectual level of critique but also at the imaginative level of wonderment and, finally, silence.

The final section of the *Phaedo* recounts the last exchange between Socrates and Crito. Though his devotion to his friend is indisputable, Crito is someone who never quite comprehends Socrates' meaning. He involves himself in the humdrum, minutiae of Socrates' life, missing its wider import. He never quite sees the wood for the trees. If we recall the sisters of Lazarus in the Gospel, Crito is like Martha who prepared the food, whilst Plato is like Mary who sat at the master's feet.

So it is not surprising when, at the last, Crito asks Socrates what practical instructions he has for his followers, in relation to his children perhaps, or anything else. 'Nothing new,' Socrates replies warmly:

> But what I am always saying, that you will please me and mine and yourselves by taking good care of your own selves in whatever you do, even if you do not agree with me now. But if you neglect your own selves, and are unwilling to live following the tracks, as it were, of what we have said now and on previous occasions, you will achieve nothing.

To follow in Socrates' tracks is not to agree or disagree with him. It is to seriously and searchingly care for oneself in the sum total of one's being.

Q - IS A QUESTION

One of the best articulations of the religious attitude is provided by Augustine, who asks in his *Confessions*, 'What do I love when I love my God?' He was a Christian, of course. He believed that God had spoken to him and, once converted, he turned much of his energy to fleshing out what it meant to give assent to faith and doctrine. However, inasmuch as Christians and agnostics share a common religious sensibility, he expresses the aspiration to know what it is to love the unknown God famously well. What does he love when he loves God?

> Not material beauty or the beauty of a temporal order; not the brilliance of earthly light, so welcome to our eyes; not the sweet melody of harmony and song; not the fragrance of flowers, perfumes, and spices; not manna or honey; not limbs such as the body delights to embrace. It is not these that I love when I love my God.

And yet, when I love him, it is true that I love a light of a certain kind, a voice, a perfume, a food, an embrace; but they are the
kind that I love in my inner self, when my soul is bathed in light
that is not bound by space; when it listens to sound that never dies
away; when it breathes fragrance that is not borne away on the
wind; when it tastes food that is never consumed by the eating;
when it clings to an embrace from which it is not severed by ful-
fillment of desire. This is what I love when I love my God.

So what is my God?, Augustine finally asks: creation, existence, wonderment, silence. 'I asked these questions simply by gazing at these
things, and their beauty was all the answer they gave.' No more - but no
less either. This is the possibility of God.

R - IS FOR READING AND WRITING

Plato was wary of writing. He suspected that, in the way it objectified
philosophy, it could become an excuse not to live it. He thought that, in
the way it tidied philosophy up, it could become a means of concealing
meaning that can only be experienced. So convinced was he of this risk
that in the *Republic*, he bans poets from his model city-state. It seems an
extreme position to adopt. But poets were authority figures. The body
of work from Hesiod to Homer people remembered and recited, and in
Plato's time had started to write down, was the dogmatic canon of the
day. The danger is that poets would appeal to the dogmatic instincts of
citizens in providing a ready-made source of knock-out proof-texts for
the positions they opposed.

These days the best novels are quasi-religious texts. Jeannette
Winterson, an author who has been accused of deliberately confusing literature and religion, wrote in an article for the London *Times* (available on
her website): 'If you believe, as I do, that life has an inside as well as an
outside, you will accept that the inner life needs nourishment too. If the
inner life is not supported and sustained, then there is nothing between
us and the daily repetition of what Wordsworth called "getting and spending." ' She is conscious of the differences between religion and art, 'having
spent most of my early life in a gospel tent with a pair of evangelical

parents', as she puts it. However, art is religious in a deeper sense: 'It asks us to see differently, think differently, challenging ourselves, and the way we live.' In other words, writers and artists should aim not to tie things up, but to open things out. It is an agnostic imperative that is pursued.

How have writers overcome the dangers Plato highlights that would close literature down? Shakespeare is a pivotal figure in this. Stephen Greenblatt, in his book *Will in the World*, puts his finger on a key moment. He explains how, in *Hamlet*, the playwright discovered a new device for portraying interiority on the stage. It not only elicited a passionate response in audiences. With it, he could sustain, throughout the course of a whole play, the sense in which we are unknown to ourselves.

Greenblatt calls this device opacity. It is not a deliberate obfuscation, for that would only create a frustratingly baffling piece of work. Rather, it is a persistent refusal of the rationales, motivations and ethical justifications that the playwright typically built into the morality tales of his day, and which real people have deployed to understand their own lives before and since. Shakespeare, I would say, has before him the Socratic conviction of knowing mostly of his ignorance. His genius is to know how to turn that ignorance over and over again in the characters, images, echoes and plots of his plays. The reason why this opacity works so astonishingly well on stage is that it reflects our own inability to know ourselves. Greenblatt adds the speculation that Shakespeare's discovery of this device was intimately connected to the agnostic character of his own life - 'his skepticism, his pain, his sense of broken rituals, his refusal of easy consolations'.

King Lear is the most striking example of opacity. As soon as the story begins it does not make sense. Lear asks his daughters how much they love him, so that he can divide his kingdom accordingly. Not only is the kingdom already divided but the question itself is meaningless. Lear's own unfathomable needs are exposed. When Cordelia replies, 'Nothing', it fills him with dread, a fear that grows to the tragic climax of the play. Why does he go mad? Perhaps because he is giving up the crown. Perhaps because he is old. We never know for sure because there is no sure reason to be had.

The refusal to settle things is common in many great works of literature. The result is, of course, not always tragic. Proust's *In Search of Lost Time*, never quite gets to the bottom of of it all. But we learn an enormous amount about paying attention to life in the process.

S - IS FOR SILENCE

'Under all speech that is good for anything there lies a silence that is better.' Thomas Carlyle.

T - IS ABOUT THERAPY

Foucault noticed that it was early Christianity which first instigated a practice of self-examination that required the individual to examine their inner life and reveal it to another - that practice being the confession of the penitent to a wiser confessor. What is doubly interesting about confession is that it presupposes that the penitent might easily deceive themselves. They might confess one sin that was actually symptomatic of another; so penitents must not just confess but actively search their souls. It was in this capacity that the wise confessor was so important. Their role was to exercise discernment, thereby steering the penitent in the direction that would reveal the greatest truths about themselves. The goal was change. In bringing failures to light, confession was connected to the proleptic promise of baptism; penitents were 'putting on salvation'.

Sadly, Foucault thought, this exercise of personal transformation was itself transformed as the Church became a dogmatic institution. With the need to manage the souls of millions, confession became a sort of check-list exercise. In confession, the penitent did not search their souls but ticked off the sins they had committed in order to be restored to the Church. The role of the confessor was not so much to nurture change as exercise what Foucault called 'pastoral power'.

Psychoanalysts exercise a secular version of confession. Whether it be in the making of connections between the free associations of the client or offering insights that the client would never have been conscious of themselves, the pattern is the same. The truth is found within and it is discovered by speaking it out. Eventually, the analysand will reach a point at which all their confusions, neuroses, rationalisations and delusions will have been exposed to the light of day. Their analysis will be complete.

I remember a psychoanalyst once telling me that she was nearing the end of her therapy. I was fascinated by the idea. What would that be like - perhaps enlightened, or wholly conscious, or supremely in control, or in a state of maximal closure? When I asked, she laughed and replied nothing like that at all. All that the completion of her analysis signified was that she and her therapist had done all the work together that they possibly could. When I jested that it seemed to me that there must be more work for her to do, she pointed out that I did not know her before she started the therapy!

The point is that therapy does not aim at the resolution of all problems, complete knowledge of oneself, or even the increase in happiness, though it might well help someone to manage a debilitating neurosis. Therapy brings one to the limits of what can be known and understood about oneself. In this sense, the end of one's analysis is the start of a life aware of one's ignorance. The direction that any one individual chooses to take after that will vary. For Nietzsche, having undergone a therapy of writing in his so-called middle-period books, the next step was to develop the will to live in spite of what he had concluded about the nature of existence. He created the heroic character of Zarathustra to explore what that might mean. For the Christian, as John Cottingham explains in *The Spiritual Dimension*: 'Dependency, vulnerability, the insistence that strength is made perfect in weakness, are the hallmarks of the Judaeo-Christian spiritual tradition (and perhaps the key Islamic notion of *submission* says something not too dissimilar).'

Jonathan Lear believes that Freud can be read as providing an answer to the Socratic question of how one should live and the intuition that it begins with knowing oneself. The problem, as Socrates himself knew, is that people readily deceive themselves. Like prisoners in a cave confusing shadows with reality, they would prefer to think that they know the meaning of things and that they understand their own nature. Admitting ignorance, they suppose, would be to condemn humankind to its self-delusion, lost like the blind leading the blind. Freud's way out of this fix was to devise a way of talking that borrowed from the early Christian tradition of radical uncertainty about oneself. Socrates

Illus. 7.2:   Sigmund Freud's 'royal road' to the unknown unconscious borrows from the Christian tradition of radical uncertainty.

founded his philosophy on a practice that is recognisably similar. He developed the habit of persistently asking questions of himself and others that revolved around a central conviction: 'I am very conscious that I am not wise at all.'

U - IS FOR THE UNORTHODOX

Some of the greatest religious spirits have been heretics - not least, the founders of the great religions!

W - IS FOR WHY?

Meaning is nothing if not subjective. This is the fundamental reason that the scientific worldview, for all it unpicks, does not do, nor deliver, meaning of itself. It sits on the wrong side of the subject/object, fact/value, material/spiritual divide. The Faustian pact with which our world flirts is trusting the results of science and its method above all others for fixing truths. The paradox is that this culture of certainty produces anxiety because, at the end of the day, to be certain is to be in denial. Thus we live more healthily but not more happily; we live more magnificently but not more meaningfully; we live with more knowledge but not more wisdom.

Secular philosophies suggest that meaning can be found within this frame nonetheless. One possibility is to argue that the big questions of life are overblown or mistaken. The moral imperative of how one should live should be rephrased to the more manageable one of how one might become more cultivated, more ethical or simply less demanding of life. The task of knowing thyself is mitigated by the commonsensical comment that most of the time, in most situations, one probably knows oneself enough to get on with matters in hand. When climactic moments come, like death, one should just accept them, not question them.

Faith offers another possibility as a source of meaning. The thought here is that, if meaning is subjective, then for it to rest assured, there must be an absolute source of subjectivity for it to rest assured on, namely, the personal God. Some believe that this 'meaning of meaning' is manifest in the Bible or the Church. Other more subtle believers would say that it emerges like shapes in the dark: that it seems shadowy is merely a reflection of our inability to see clearly, not of its objective reality.

Agnosticism offers another possibility: meaning as mystery. At one level, this is almost to assert a cliché. It is not unless one is prepared to 'step out into the unknown' that one's life expands, deepens and grows. Similarly, it might be thought close to tautologous: '[The] ultimate springs and principles are totally shut up from human curiosity and enquiry,' was Hume's nonnegotiable phrase, implying that meaning, inasmuch as it depends only these ultimate things, will remain mysterious too.

However, the mystery of agnosticism is not simply an impasse. It is a quest. Meaning is not found by dwelling in the regions that one believes one understands, and erecting walls around them, material or metaphysical, in order to pretend they are all that is. Paradoxically perhaps, the desire for meaning is satisfied by dwelling on the thresholds of ignorance.

Not that any old mystification will do! The tradition that began with Socrates offers a way that is practical as well as contemplative. Here was a man who though claiming to know nothing could never have been accused of having a black hole at the heart of his life. No-one was wiser than he, not because he was wise, but because he loved more powerfully and penetratingly what most only long for to a degree. He stirred those around him into life by irony, argument and example, and mostly by the encounter with his passion and love.

Y - IS FOR YOU

'Know thyself!' Delphic inscription.

Z - IS UNENDING

I searched the writings of Zeno and Zohar for the final letter of the alphabet. Zeno's paradoxes have thrown many onto the limits of reason, with the infinities he found in finite space. And Zohar the Kabbalist is full of agnostic sentiments: 'If a man thinks that the garment is the actual Torah itself, and not something quite other, may his spirit depart, and may he have no portion in the world to come.' But perhaps it can be used to reflect that, if Z is the last letter of the alphabet, there is no end to the agnostic quest.

FURTHER READING AND REFERENCES

INTRODUCTION

Friedrich Schleiermacher discusses his religious sensibility in *On Religion: Speeches to Its Cultured Despisers*. Paul Tillich presents his ontology in Volume I, Part II of his *Systematic Theology*. Accessible sermons are also available in collections.

Nietzsche's announcement of the death of God comes in *The Gay Science*, Book 3, 125, translated by Walter Kaufman and published by Vintage Books (1974).

True Religion, by Graham Ward, published by Blackwell (2003), examines why the emergence of the scientific worldview is not the end of religion but the remaking of it.

Karen Armstrong discusses the birth of American fundamentalism and figures like A. C. Dixon in *The Battle for God: Fundamentalism in Judaism, Christianity and Islam*, published by Harper Collins (2000), see page 178-9.

T. H. Huxley's essay 'Agnosticism' can be found in the misleadingly entitled *Atheism: a Reader*, edited by S. T. Joshi, published by Prometheus Books (2000), see page 33 for the quote.

God's Funeral, by A. N. Wilson, published by Abacus (1999), sets Victorian agnosticism in a wider historical context.

Scholarly studies on Victorian agnosticism include:

The Unbelievers: English Agnostic Thought, by A. O. J. Cockshutt (Collins: 1964) - a good survey of players.

The Origins of Agnosticism: Victorian Unbelief and the Limits of Knowledge, by Bernard Lightman (Johns Hopkins University Press, 1987) - good on agnosticism's relationship to the philosophy of Kant and why Victorian agnosticism as a movement died.

Søren Kierekegaard's *Fear and Trembling* is a Penguin Classic, translated by Alastair Hannay (1985): see page 62 for the quote.

All the quotes from Plato are taken from *Plato Complete Works*, edited by John M. Cooper, published by Hackett Publishing Company (1997). The quote from the *Phaedrus* is at 278d.

1. SOCRATES' QUEST: THE BEGINNING OF WISDOM

Greek Religion, by Walter Burkert, translated by John Raffan, published by Blackwell (1985), is the standard text on the eponymous subject.

The Religion of Socrates, by Mark L. McPherran, published by Penn State University Press (1996), is the most thorough examination of the historical Socrates' attitude and feelings about religion and belief that I have seen.

The quote from the *Laws* is at 948c.

Xenophon's Socratic 'proof' for the existence of gods is in his *Memoirs of Socrates* 1.4.
The account of Socrates' response to the oracle begins at *Apology* 20e.
Plutarch's account of Socrates' peripatetic method is in *Whether a Man Should Engage in Politics when He Is Old*, 26, 796d.
The discussion about gods and goodness (or piety) begins around *Euthyphro* 9c.
Diotima's contribution in the *Symposium* begins at 201d. Alcibiades appears at 212d.
The interview with Bertrand Russell is reprinted in *Russell on Religion: Selections from the Writings of Bertrand Russell*, published by Routledge (1999), Chapter 4, 'What Is an Agnostic?'.
The Road to Delphi: the Life and Afterlife of Oracles, by Michael Wood, published by Picador (2003), is a fascinating and evocative study of the role of ancient oracles.

2. COSMOLOGISTS AND DARWINISTS: THE LIMITS OF SCIENCE

Newton: the Making of Genius, by Patricia Fara is published by Picador (2003).
The Philosophy of Science: a Very Short Introduction, by Samir Okasha, published by Oxford University Press (2002), does what it says on the cover.
Thomas Kuhn's revolutionary ideas are in his 1963 book *The Structure of Scientific Revolutions* (University of Chicago Press).
Karl Popper's revolutionary ideas are in his 1959 book *The Logic of Scientific Discovery* (Hutchinson).
A very useful summary of issues in the philosophy of science comes from a discussion Brian Magee had with Hilary Putnam, reproduced in *Talking Philosophy*, published by Oxford University Press (1978), Chapter 12, from which the Putnam quotes are taken.
Kuhn vs Popper: the Struggle for the Soul of Science, by Steve Fuller is published by Icon (2003).
The quote of Werner Heisenberg is from his *Physics and Philosophy*, published by Penguin Books (1989), on page 167.
Our Final Century? Will the Human Race Survive the 21st Century?, by Martin Rees is published by Arrow (2004).
Richard Dawkins's essay 'The Sacred and the Scientist' is in Ben Rogers's *Is Nothing Sacred?*, published by Routledge (2004), with the quote on page 137.
The Story of God, by Robert Winston, is published by Bantam Press (2005).

3. VISIONS OF REALITY: SCIENCE AND WONDER

All that remains of the writings of the pre-Socratic philosophers are in *Early Greek Philosophy*, published by Penguin Classics (2001), with introductory material by Jonathan Barnes. Empedocles' 'Twofold Tale' is on pages 120-2.
Socrates tells of his change from natural science to philosophy beginning at *Phaedo* 96a.
Happiness: Lessons from a New Science, by Richard Layard, is published by Allen Lane (2005).
An example of the distinction between *zoē* and *bios* is deployed by Aristotle in his *Politics*, see 1252b30.
Susan Greenfield made her point about asking the right questions of neuroscience at an event entitled 'Religion and Neuroscience' at the Royal Institution in May 2005.

Michael Atiyah deployed his metaphor of the Faustian pact in a lecture given in 2000 entitled 'Mathematics in the Twentieth Century'. It has been reproduced in *Mathematical Association of America Monthly*, August-September 2001.

Brian Ridley's *On Science* is published by Routledge (2001), see pages 46 and 141 for the quotes.

TechGnosis, by Erik Davis, published by Harmony Books (1998), has more on the importing of the religious imagination into science.

The Essential Mary Midgley, edited by David Midgley, is published by Routledge (2005) and provides an excellent survey of her work. See 'Salvation and the Academics', pages 228-38, for her reflections on DNA.

Dominique Janicaud's *On the Human Condition* is published by Routledge (2002), see pages 54-8.

'Life', by Samuel Taylor Coleridge, is in *Selected Poetry*, edited by Richard Holmes, published by Penguin Books (1996), page 8.

Moby Dick, by Herman Melville, is a Penguin Classic (2003). The quotes are in Chapter 42, 'The Whiteness of the Whale', page 206.

Longinus, 'On Sublimity', is in *Classical Literary Criticism*, published by Oxford University Press (1989), page 143.

David Attenborough made his comments to the press when *Life in the Undergrowth* was launched.

Thomas Traherne's thoughts on flies and celestial strangers are in the excellent anthology *Thomas Traherne Poetry and Prose*, selected and introduced by Denise Inge, published by SPCK (2002), pages 111-14.

Baron von Hügel's comments are quoted in a review of his *The Reality of God, and Religion and Agnosticism*, in the *Times Literary Supplement* of Thursday, 18 June 1931.

Roger Scruton discusses piety in *An Intelligent Person's Guide to Philosophy*, published by Penguin Books (1996), see page 117.

Einstein's relevant writings and thoughts are all gathered at www.einsteinandreligion.com, including these quotes.

Piers Benn's essay 'The Idea of the Sacred' appears in Ben Rogers's *Is Nothing Sacred?* (see above), quote on page 126.

The *Devout Sceptics* interviews by Bel Mooney are collected in a Hodder and Stoughton book with the same title (2003): see page 57 for Paul Davies's quote.

4. BAD FAITH: RELIGION AS CERTAINTY

Atheism: a Very Short Introduction, by Julian Baggini, is published by Oxford University Press (2003): see page 106 for the quote. In *What's It All About? Philosophy and the Meaning of Life*, published by Granta (2004), he offers an atheist's take on the 'big questions'.

Denys Turner's lecture 'How to Be an Atheist' is in his collected talks *Faith Seeking*, published by SCM Press (2002).

Philosophy: the Latest Answers to the Oldest Questions, by Nicholas Fearn, is published by Atlantic Books (2005).

Herbert McCabe is quoted in *The Thought of Thomas Aquinas*, by Brian Davies, published by Clarendon Paperbacks (1993), page 111.

Karen Armstrong discusses her ideas on *logos* and myth in *The Battle for God* (see above). A concise version is in *A Short History of Myth*, published by Canongate (2005): see page 122 for quote.

Serious Concerns, by Wendy Cope, is published by Faber and Faber (1992).

Disciplining the Divine: the Failure of the Social Model of the Trinity, by Paul Fletcher, is published by Ashgate (forthcoming).

No God But God: the Origins, Evolution and Future of Islam, by Reza Alsan, is published William Heinemann (2005), see page 263 for quote.

5. CHRISTIAN AGNOSTICISM:
LEARNED IGNORANCE

The story about Thomas Aquinas is in Brian Davies's *The Thought of Thomas Aquinas* (see above).

De docta ignorantia, by Nicholas of Cusa, is available online. This quote comes in Chapter 1, 'How it is that knowing is not-knowing'.

The quote from Meister Eckhart is from his sermon XCIX, available in collected works.

The Unknown God: Agnostic Essays, by Anthony Kenny, is published by Continuum (2004), with his reflections on Arthur Hugh Clough's poem in Chapter 1, 'The Ineffable Godhead': see page 20 for the quote. Chapter 8 compares Clough and Arnold.

T. H. Huxley's reflections were in a review of *Agnosticism* published in the *Times Literary Supplement* of Friday, 27 February 1903.

6. FOLLOWING SOCRATES: A WAY
OF LIFE

The discussion of Plato's Academy in Chapter 4 of *Plato: an Introduction*, by Paul Friedländer, published by Princeton University Press (1973) and translated by Hans Meyerhoff is fairly old now but is hard to beat.

The Seneca quote is from *Moral Epistles* 6, 6.

The Plato quote from the *Seventh Letter* is at 341c.

Pierre Hadot's idea of philosophy as a way of life is developed in several books. An accessible text is *What Is Ancient Philosophy?*, published by Harvard University Press (2002). The quote I use can be found on page 62 of this book.

Philosophy as a Way of Life: Spiritual Exercises from Socrates to Foucault, edited with an introduction by Arnold I. Davidson and translated by Michael Chase, published by Blackwell (1995), develops the idea further.

The Art of Living: Socratic Reflections from Plato to Foucault, by Alexander Nehamas, published by University of California Press (1998), is also fascinating.

Plato's myth in the *Gorgias* begins at 523a.

Aristotle's characterisation of the wise man is in his *Nicomachean Ethics* 1125a12.

The quote from Montaigne is in his essay 'On educating children' (I: 26). *The Complete Essays*, translated by M. A. Screech, is published by Penguin Classics. The quote is on page 180.

D. H. Lawrence's essay 'The Good Man' is discussed by Christopher Hamilton in his *Living Philosophy: Reflections on Life, Meaning and Morality*, published by Edinburgh University Press (2001), on page 122. The original quote is in Lawrence, *Phoenix I*, edited by D. McDonald (Heinemann, 1961), page 752.

A summary of Michel Foucault's idea of thinking differently is in the introduction to the second volume of his History of Sexuality, *The Use of Pleasure*. The seminar he gave on 6 January 1982, transcribed in *The Hermeneutics of the Subject: Lectures at the Collège de France 1981-1982*, published by Palgrave Macmillan (2005), focusses on the relationship between Christian and ancient philosophical moral practice. Some of the interviews in *Foucault: Live Collected Interviews, 1961-1984,* edited by Sylvère Lotringer (Semiotext [e], 1996), are also illuminating.

Essays and Aphorisms, by Arthur Schopenhauer, with an introduction by R. J. Hollingdale, published by Penguin Classics (1970), is a good introduction to his thought and way of life. Schopenhauer's equivocation about whether philosophy can change a life is discussed in *Schopenhauer,* by Julian Young, published by Routledge (2005), on pages 158-64.

Bryan Magee writes about knowing Karl Popper in his *Confessions of a Philosopher: a Journey through Western Philosophy,* published by Phoenix (1997). Popper on Socrates is discussed on page 561.

Unended Quest, by Karl Popper, is published by Routledge (1992), with the quote about happiness on page 145.

On Religion, by John Caputo, is published by Routledge (2001).

7. HOW TO BE AN AGNOSTIC: AN APHORISTIC A-Z

The Owl of Minerva: a Memoir, by Mary Midgley, is published by Routledge (2005). The quote is on page x.

The Daniel J. Boorstin quote is from an essay 'The Amateur Spirit', in *Living Philosophies,* edited by C. Fadiman, published by Doubleday (1990).

The Francis Bacon quote is from *The Advancement of Learning,* published in 1605.

A summary of Karl Popper on Darwinism is in *Unended Quest,* Chapter 37 (see above).

Melvyn Bragg's quote is in *Devout Sceptics* (see above).

Oscar Wilde's essay can be found in his collected works.

John Elliot Gardner made this comment in an interview on the BBC's *Front Row* with Mark Lawson.

Roger Hull makes his comments on the American Sublime in the catalogue to the exhibition.

Leslie Stephen's *An Agnostic's Apology* is in *Atheism: a Reader* (see above).

Augustine ponders the question 'What do I love when I love my God?' in Book X.6 of his *Confessions.* The quote is from the translation by R. S. Pine-Coffin, published by Penguin Books (1961).

Freud, by Jonathan Leer, is published by Routledge (2005).

Jeannette Winterson's website is www.jeannettewinterson.com.

Will in the World, by Stephen Greenblatt, is published by Pimlico (2004).

Thomas Carlyle's quote on silence is in his essay 'Sir Walter Scott', in *Critical and Miscellaneous Essays.*

The Spiritual Dimension: Religion, Philosophy and Human Value, by John Cottingham, is published by Cambridge University Press (2005).

INDEX